CurriCULum Focus

Famous Events

John Davis

HOPSCOTCH
H
EDUCATIONAL PUBLISHING

Curriculum Focus series

History

Toys Key Stage 1
Famous Events Key Stage 1
Famous People Key Stage 1
Invaders Key Stage 2
Tudors Key Stage 2

Geography

Islands and Seasides Key Stage 1
The Local Area Key Stage 1

Science

Ourselves Key Stage 1
Plants and Animals Key Stage 1
Materials Key Stage 1

Published by Hopscotch Educational Publishing Ltd,
Unit 2, The Old Brushworks, 56 Pickwick Road,
Corsham, Wiltshire SN13 9BX
Tel: 01249 701701

© 2004 Hopscotch Educational Publishing

Written by John Davis
Linked ICT activities by Michelle Singleton
Series design by Blade Communications
Illustrations by Sarah Wimperis, Dave Burroughs and
Tony Randell
Cover illustration by Susan Hutchison
Printed by Colorman (Ireland) Ltd

John Davis hereby asserts his moral right to be identified
as the author of this work in accordance with the
Copyright, Designs and Patents Act, 1988.

ISBN1-904307-30-2

Contents

Cross-curricular links

Chapter	History SoW	PSHE/Citizenship SoW	Literacy framework	ICT SoW
1	Unit 5		Y2, Term 1: S4 Y2, Term 2: S7 Y2, Term 2: S9	Units 1B, 1C, 2A, 2B,
2	Unit 5		Y2, Term 1: S4	Units 1C, 1E, 2B
3	Unit 5	Units 1 and 2	Y2, Term 1: S4 Y2, Term 2: S7	Units 1B, 2A, 2B
4	Unit 5		Y2, Term 2: S7 Y2, Term 2: S9 Speaking & Listening KS1	Units 1B, 1C

Introduction

One of the most important ways laid down for Key Stage 1 children to be introduced to history is through the study of past events from the history of Britain and the wider world.

Such a study can help them learn the vocabulary of history, highlight the differences between then and now and teach them how we know about what has happened in the past. Furthermore, it challenges them to think about the questions people ask about events in the past and assists them to understand the concepts of chronology and change.

The purpose of this comprehensive resource – one of the Curriculum Focus: History series – is to incorporate all these elements and to inspire teachers, especially the non-specialist, to teach history with confidence.

The four events covered in the book are the Great Fire of London, the Olympic Games, The Gunpowder Plot and Coronation Day. The first of these is featured in the QCA's Scheme of Work for History Unit 5. The others have been specially chosen for the links they have with ancient history and regular modern events (the Olympics), annual seasonal festivals (Bonfire Night) and recent celebrations within the lifetime of Key Stage 1 children (the Golden Jubilee of Queen Elizabeth II). The book is also intended to be flexible enough to integrate with any schools' own scheme of work or to be dipped into as and when required.

- Each chapter contains extensive background information about the topic written at the teachers' level and photocopiable resources providing stimulating pictures, maps, diagrams and charts.

- This is followed by three detailed lesson plans on the theme, each based on clear historical objectives. Resources are listed and starting points for the whole class are outlined. Lesson plans are largely organised in a question and answer format to provide essential information and assist with the teaching process.

- The group activities that follow are based on highly practical differentiated photocopiable

tasks at three ability levels that reinforce and develop the content of the lesson. Guidance is given about how children can be prepared for these activities and how they might be organised and supported.

- The main points of the lesson are revisited in plenary sessions that are interactive and often include drama and role play.

- At the end of each chapter there are ideas for support and extension and suggestions are made for linking aspects of ICT into the work.

The Great Fire of London

Background

All large cities like London experienced outbreaks of fire during the seventeenth century but nothing was to prepare England's largest settlement for the disaster that struck in 1666.

It was very much a case of lightning striking in the same place twice, for only the previous year over 68,000 of the capital's population had been wiped out by a virulent attack of bubonic plague.

London at this time had a population of about 460,000 people. In Europe, only the size of Paris was greater. The only route across the River Thames was London Bridge. Regions like Kensington and Chelsea were still regarded as separate villages. Most of those living in the central areas were packed into the decaying wooden houses that crammed the narrow streets. Rubbish thrown out from houses, shops and warehouses was collected by workmen called 'scavengers' but was thrown into the river or piled up outside the city walls. It was the perfect breeding ground for rats and other vermin.

The Plague – spread by fleas that lived on infected rats – began in the winter of 1664. As the spring of the following year developed into summer and the weather became hotter, it began to take its hold on the city. By mid-July 1,000 people were dying each week and still the situation worsened. Whole families who showed symptoms of the disease were boarded up inside their houses and watchmen were appointed to keep them in. The bodies of the dead were transported away during the hours of darkness, many to be buried in mass graves.

Some inhabitants tried to escape the city into the surrounding countryside, but the residents of neighbouring settlements were understandably unwilling to accept them. Others lived on boats anchored in the middle of the River Thames. King Charles II and the court fled to Oxford and did not return until the worst was over. The death rate reached its peak during September when over 26,000 people died. As winter approached the situation began to improve, although it was only towards Christmas that life began to get back to normal.

The fire

Tradition locates the origin of the Great Fire in the bakery run by Thomas Farynor in Pudding Lane some time early in the morning of Sunday 2 September. The likely cause seems to be that the fires that operated the baking ovens had not been properly put out when the baker, his family and the servants retired to bed. Farynor and the immediate members of his family are said to have escaped the burning building by jumping from an upstairs window, but a maid could not be persuaded to get out by using this method and died.

The summer of 1666 had been long and hot, so neighbouring buildings caught fire quickly and the flames were fanned by a keen east wind, which also carried sparks a considerable distance. By 7am some 300 houses had been destroyed and chaos reigned in the streets as people attempted to escape across the river. As the end of the day came, the blaze stretched a distance of over a mile.

By Monday 3 September the fire had reached the centre of the city, particularly the business area around the Royal Exchange. The streets were now jammed with people pushing handcarts and barrows laden with goods as they tried to save what they could of their possessions. Escape across the river became more difficult as London Bridge had become an early victim of the flames. The following day is often known as 'terrible Tuesday' with half the city now ravaged by fire. Cheapside, the capital's main shopping area, was destroyed as well as the Guildhall, the main centre of local government, and Fleet Street. Also to suffer at this point was St Paul's Cathedral, one of the most prominent landmarks in the whole of the city. The blaze had reached the Temple area and Cripplegate by Wednesday, but then it began to abate as the wind dropped and fire-fighting teams began to have some effect. The fire finally stopped its progress at Pye Corner.

After the flames and the smoke gradually died away on Thursday, the city slowly began to return to normal. But it was not until the weekend or early the following week that people began to return from the fields outside the city where they had set up their temporary and makeshift homes. Many writers commented on the help given to Londoners by those living in neighbouring settlements. Accounts describe how they provided shelter wherever possible and lent out transport – carts, wagons and coaches – that could be used for saving possessions.

Fire fighting

Fire fighting in seventeenth-century London can be described as primitive at best. Hand pumps and squirts were used to put out small flames, or residents formed chains to pass buckets of water obtained from the nearest river or pond. Hooked poles, axes and chains were used for pulling down burning thatch or on occasions demolishing whole houses. A supply of these was kept in each city ward.

The only other method used to stop a major fire was to create a gap too big for the flames to cross by blowing up buildings with a charge of gunpowder. The Tower of London was one of many buildings saved in this way.

With the fire breaking out during the night, few people were alert enough to deal with it quickly. By the time the Lord Mayor, Thomas Bludworth, began to organise teams of fire-fighters the following day, the blaze already had a firm grip. Later, despite being given orders by Pepys from the King, Bludworth was reluctant to blow up houses and this only made the situation worse. The whole fire-fighting operation was plagued by the fact that no one appeared to be willing to take sole responsibility. Attempts to combat the flames were further hampered by the fact that the blazing banks of the River Thames cut off fire-fighters from the city's only plentiful supply of water.

Prominent in the fire-fighting operation was both the King and his brother James, the Duke of York. They stood ankle deep in water on the front line, encouraging teams of soldiers, sailors and parish constables to tackle the flames and smoke as best they could.

Surveying the damage

When the final cost of the fire damage was surveyed, London reeled in horror.

- Over half the total area within the city walls, some 15 hectares, had been totally destroyed.
- Outside the city wall, 25 hectares had also been severely damaged.
- Over 13,000 houses on some 400 streets had gone up in flames.
- Over 80 churches and most of the larger public buildings in the city had disappeared.
- 100,000 people had been made homeless and were forced to spend the winter of 1666 in tents and shelters until their homes were rebuilt.
- The estimated cost of damage to property and goods was put at £10 million – a staggering amount of money for those times.
- At its peak, the fire is said to have produced flames up to 100 metres high and the glow could be seen for miles around.
- Mercifully, because most inhabitants fled rather than staying to fight the fire, only eight people died.

The rebuilding operation

Although some of the worst areas of London remained intact, the Great Fire did help to purify some places of the last remains of the Plague and it did provide the opportunity for large stretches of the capital city to be rebuilt. A number of grandiose plans were put forward for the rebuilding, including those by Evelyn and the architect Sir Christopher Wren, but none was fully adopted.

The building programme started slowly. Despite an influx of skilled building workers, only 150 premises had been completed by 1667. This had risen to about 9,000 by 1671 although many of them remained empty. A special Fire Court set up to handle disputes about property rights and boundaries did not conclude its business until 1673. Some progress was hampered by the fact that many people were resistant to change and wanted to return to houses similar to those they had occupied before the fire. New rules governed the building of houses, streets became wider, squares were created, pavements provided and new drains installed. Brick, stone and tile became the predominant building materials in the place of wood and thatch. The West End of London, close to the palaces and parks, became the centre for the wealthy while the East End, with its cheap rented accommodation, attracted the poor.

Wren, an Oxford professor from the age of 29 with an interest in mathematics and astronomy, established a reputation for his detailed drawings and precise models. He had survived the Plague by fleeing to Paris and after the Great Fire devoted much of his life to designing London's public buildings including the Royal Hospital, Chelsea and palaces at Kensington and Hampton Court. He became the King's Surveyor of Works in 1667. He was responsible for the rebuilding of St Paul's Cathedral and over 50 parish churches. St Paul's, the biggest cathedral in Europe apart from St Peter's in Rome, took 35 years to complete and remains Wren's greatest monument. He was knighted for his efforts in 1672.

Sources of information

Although a number of contemporary paintings, sketches and engravings of the Great Fire of London exist, most tend to focus on general scenes of the fire engulfing houses, churches and other public buildings and the chaos that ensued. Others show the exodus down the River Thames or the homeless camping in fields outside the city. Most were not genuine eyewitness accounts but were painted sometime afterwards and relied on engravings of what London had looked like before the fire took hold.

The most reliable and detailed accounts of the damage caused by the fire and the human misery it inflicted come in the writings of diarists like Samuel Pepys and John Evelyn and politicians like the Earl of Clarendon. Pepys (1633–1703) was an important government official who was promoted because of his organisational ability. His main responsibility was buying supplies for the Royal Navy. He lived within the city itself and was well placed to describe events as they unfolded. Pepys' own house was spared, although ironically it burned down in another fire seven years later. Pepys' diary – containing over a million words – was first published in 1825. It is highly regarded because of the way in which it combines small detail as well as supplying the whole picture of events. It includes details of how Pepys tried to safeguard his most treasured possessions while the fire was at its height. Initially, some of his goods, money and silverware

were moved to safety in the village of Bethnal Green – two miles east of London. Later, he took to burying items in deep holes in the ground. The most important of these items appeared to be his supply of wine and Parmesan cheese.

Evelyn (1620–1706), another prominent diarist and a lifelong friend of Pepys, lived in Fetter Lane, Holborn, and was placed in charge of the fire-fighting teams around his home. Evelyn – the author of some 30 books on the arts, forestry and religious topics – started writing his diary at the age of 11 and continued it for the rest of his life. During the Great Fire of London he wrote at some length about the destruction of St Paul's Cathedral and visited the fields outside London that had become the home of many refugees. Later he submitted plans for the rebuilding of London in which he proposed plantations of fragrant trees and shrubs around the city. He also served on several important government commissions.

The Earl of Clarendon was Lord Chancellor (in effect the Prime Minister of the day) at the time of the Great Fire. This put him in a key position to comment on the strategies being used by the city's rulers to fight the blaze. His daughter later married the King's brother, the Duke of York, and he later became the grandfather of two English monarchs, Queen Mary II and Queen Anne. Clarendon fell out of favour in 1667, was dismissed and spent the last part of his life in exile in France. Extracts from the writings of all three of these important characters are given on Generic sheet 3.

The Great Fire of London

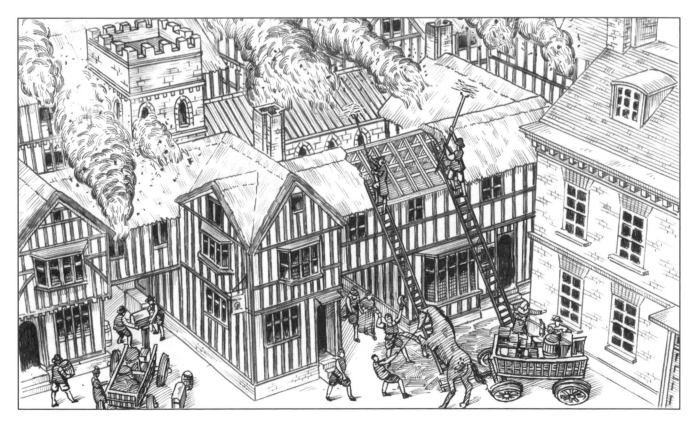

The Great Fire of London

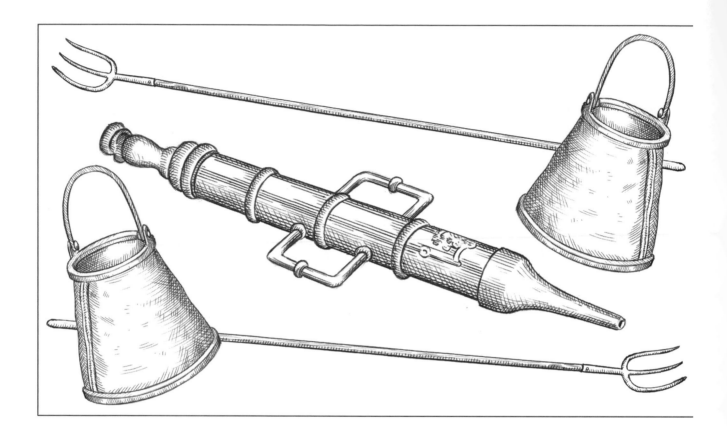

Eyewitness accounts

Samuel Pepys

Soon after the start of the fire looking out of his bedroom window:
'...being unused to such fires as followed, I thought it far enough off; and went to bed again to sleep.'

Later:
'The churches, houses and all on fire and flaming at once; and a horrid noise the flames made and the cracking of houses at their ruin.'

The Earl of Clarendon

'The fire and the wind continued in the same excess all Monday, Tuesday and Wednesday until afternoon and flung and scattered brands burning into all quarters; the nights more terrible than the days, and the light the same, the light of the fire supplying that of the sun.'

John Evelyn

How the fire got out of control:
'The conflagration was so universal and the people so astonished that from the beginning they hardly stirred to quench it, so as there was nothing heard or seen but crying out and running about like distracted creatures... The shrieking of the women and children, the hurry of people, the fall of towers, houses and churches, was like a hideous storm.'

He visits the refugees in the fields outside London:
'I then went towards Islington and Highgate where one might have seen 200,000 people of all ranks and degrees dispersed and lying along by their heaps of what they could save from the fire.'

Sir Thomas Bludworth, Lord Mayor of London

When told to destroy houses to prevent the spread of the fire:
'Lord, what can I do? I am spent; people will not obey me. I have been pulling down houses, but the fire overtakes us faster than we can do it.'

Dr Thomas Vincent, a clergyman

On the destruction of St Paul's:
'...now the lead melts and runs down, as if it had been snow before the sun; and the great beams and massy stones, with a great noise, fall upon the pavement.'

William Taswell, 15-year-old schoolboy

'The ground was so hot as almost to scorch my shoes, and the air so intensely warm that unless I had stopped some time upon Fleet Bridge to rest myself, I must have fainted under the extreme languor of my spirits.'

The Great Fire of London

John Evelyn

Christopher Wren

Samuel Pepys

King Charles II

Word bank

Sights

fire   flames   smoke   sparks   burning   blowing   billowing

smouldering   glowing   illuminating   houses   churches   cathedral

plaster   timber-framed   thatch   damage   destruction   spoil   ruin

Sounds

roaring   cracking   tumbling   running   dashing   escaping   screaming

shouting   crying   rampaging   exploding   howling   splashing

sloshing   spraying

Smells

burned   charred   nasty   reek   fumes   choking   coughing

wheezing   spluttering   gasping   scorching

Questions and answers

- **Where did the fire start?** A baker's shop in Pudding Lane.

- **When did it start?** Late on Saturday 1 September, 1666 or early Sunday 2 September.

- **Why did it start?** The most likely cause was that the fire for the baking ovens was not properly put out when the household went to bed.

- **What parts of London did the fire spread to?** Over half the total area inside the city walls was totally destroyed and much else damaged by the fire. Parts outside the city walls were also severely damaged.

- **What famous buildings were damaged or destroyed?** Over 80 churches, but the most famous structures were St Paul's Cathedral, the Guildhall and London Bridge – the only route across the River Thames at that time.

- **When did the King and members of the royal family get involved?** Almost right from the start the King and his brother James, the Duke of York, were seen in the streets organising fire-fighting operations. They did not run away and leave the city as they had done during the time of the Plague.

- **Where did the people living in London go to escape the fire?** Some to churches because they were made of stone, others to the river because it was water. Many fled to the fields surrounding London to live in makeshift tents.

- **When did the fire end?** It started to die down on Thursday 4 September and was more or less out by the following day.

- **When did the fire end?** At Pye Corner.

- **Why did it end?** The wind stopped and fire-fighting began to have some effect as more people came to help. Successful tactics were used, especially the creation of fire breaks by pulling houses down or blowing them up with gunpowder.

- **When did people return to their homes?** During the weekend or early the following week (for those who still had homes).

- **What were the results of the fire?** Many parts of London were rebuilt, with wider streets, better pavements and drains. Public buildings and churches like St Paul's were replaced, designed by architects including Christopher Wren.

- **Why is it called the Great Fire of London?** London has not experienced a worse fire before or since, not even during the Blitz in the Second World War.

- **What materials were most of the houses made from?** From a wooden frame with plaster filled in between. Roofs were thatched. Furniture would be made from wood.

- **What would churches have been built from?** These, along with large public buildings, were made from stone with tiled roofs.

- **How wide were the streets?** They were very narrow. Those used by transport were about half the width of modern roads today. Back streets were only really narrow footpaths. Houses often had upper stories that jutted out so it was possible for neighbours on opposite sides of the road to reach each other through bedroom windows.

- **What kind of shops would there have been?** They were generally small, usually run from the front of a house and specialising in one item only such as baker, butcher, shoemaker, tailor, candle maker, wine merchant. Because many people could not read, shops were identified with a picture sign outside, so a baker's sign would show a loaf of bread and a shoe maker's sign would show a large boot.

- **What types of transport were there?** Most people managed on foot. Those with some money might have had a horse. Traders pushed barrows or had horse-drawn carts and wagons. The wealthy would have travelled in carriages.

Questions and answers

- **How did people get rid of rubbish?** Liquid waste was usually thrown out into the street, which had no adequate drainage system. It froze over in the winter and produced unpleasant smells during the summer. Household and shop waste was piled out into the street. Eventually it was collected by refuse workers but all they did was either dump it outside the city walls or throw it into the River Thames where some sank and some was carried further downstream.

- **Why did the fire spread so quickly in these streets?** It was a combination of factors including piles of rubbish in the streets, wooden buildings, the closeness of houses, the recent spell of dry weather and a strong wind that carried sparks from one house to another.

- **How did people react?** There was panic as people tried to get away. Few stayed to help fight the fire. That was another reason why it took so long to put out. Some tried to take their most important possessions with them either by carrying them or on carts and wagons. Others, like Samuel Pepys, dug deep holes in the ground and buried what they wanted to save. Pepys was keen to protect his wine supply and cheeses.

- **What damage had the fire done?** See background notes for full details, but stress the fact that although thousands of buildings were destroyed there was very little loss of life. Only eight people were recorded as having died as a result of the fire. Discuss fire fighting methods such as small water pumps, chains of buckets, pulling down houses or blowing them up to create 'fire breaks'. (See Generic sheets 1 and 2.)

- **Why did it take so long to put it out?** Because the methods listed above could not cope with the rapid spread of flames and also the fact that most people ran away rather than staying to help fight the blaze.

- **Why are our cities today much safer from fire?** Factors would include rapid response by the fire service, better methods of fire proofing in building and construction, fire extinguishers and sprinklers already in some buildings, fire prevention schemes, better methods of fire fighting.

- **How are people helped if they suffer fire damage today?** They are assisted with clearing up, fire prevention advice is given, insurance companies pay out money for replacement/ rebuilding to take place (provided the owner has an insurance policy).

- **Who was Samuel Pepys?** Pepys worked in London as a government official. His main job was to buy supplies for the Royal Navy and he had the reputation of being a good communicator and organiser. He kept a detailed diary throughout the course of the Great Fire. It was first published in 1825 and has since been regarded as one of the most important eyewitness accounts of the event.

- **Who was John Evelyn?** Evelyn was put in charge of the fire-fighting teams around his home in Fetter Lane, Holborn. An author by profession, he wrote some 30 books during his lifetime on such varied subjects as the arts, forestry and religion. He kept a diary throughout his life, including during the Great Fire. The diaries were published in 1818 and included events, reports and characters from over 50 years of English life.

- **Who was the Earl of Clarendon?** This nobleman was Lord Chancellor to Charles II. This was the equivalent to the role of Prime Minister today. He played a key part in trying to organise fire fighting activities. The following year, 1667, he was sacked from his job and spent the last part of his life in exile in France.

- **Who was Sir Thomas Bludworth?** He held the post of Lord Mayor of London at the time of the fire. He was in charge of fire-fighting arrangements initially, but is often blamed for not having reacted quickly enough. As the fire got worse he was replaced by other people including the King and his brother James, Duke of York.

The Great Fire of London

History objectives
- To learn where and when the Great Fire began.
- To understand what happened in the Great Fire.

Resources

- A large map of Britain
- Pictures of modern-day London
- A simple large wall timeline showing century markers
- Portraits of Charles II
- Copies of word banks
- Scissors, glue, coloured pens and pencils, spare paper
- Generic sheets 1, 2, 5 and 7 (pages 9, 10, 11 and 15)
- Activity sheets 1–3 (pages 19–21)

Starting points: *whole class*

Tell the children details of the setting and context of the story first. Locate the position of London on the map of Britain and the children's home town/city. Display pictures of modern-day London with some of the key landmarks if possible, such as Westminster Abbey, the Houses of Parliament, the London Eye and the Monument.

Tell the children they are going to find out about a fire that happened in London a long time ago. Help them to locate the approximate position of 1666 on the large class timeline. Show them portraits of King Charles II who was the king at the time of the Great Fire (Generic sheet 5). Talk about his appearance and his clothing. Explain that the period of time in which the story is set is called 'Stuart' after Charles' family name.

Relate the story of the fire in as much detail as possible, including the main events and the main characters involved. Use the pictures on Generic sheet 1 to illustrate the story. Explain that it is believed the fire started in a baker's shop in Pudding Lane some time during the night of Saturday 1 September 1666 or the early hours of Sunday 2 September. The likely cause seems to be that the fires that operated the baking ovens had

not been properly put out when the baker, his family and the servants retired to bed.

Emphasise the sequence in which the main events happened. Once the fire, fanned by the wind and helped by the dry conditions, had taken hold of the baker's shop it soon spread to the closely packed neighbouring houses. By the time most people woke up on Monday morning the fire was heading towards the city centre. London Bridge disappeared. Tuesday 4 September was the fire's worst day with half the city in flames, including the main shopping areas and the Guildhall. On Wednesday St Paul's Cathedral was finally destroyed although there had been some success in slowing the fire down. The situation improved greatly by Thursday and by Friday movement around the city resumed slowly. Most people though did not return until the weekend or early the following week.

Ask questions to reinforce the information and check how much the children have understood (see Generic sheet 7).

Group activities

Activity sheet 1
This sheet is aimed at children who will need support with sequencing the main events of the fire. The four pictures of the Great Fire shown on the sheet are arranged in the correct sequence – the fire starting, Terrible Tuesday (London Bridge destroyed), the destruction of St Paul's and the fire dying out.

The children are asked to cut out the pictures and then find the correct caption to go with each one. The captions should be rearranged first before being stuck down. Ask the children to discuss the order with a friend. Colour can be added to the illustrations to complete the task.

Activity sheet 2

This sheet is aimed at children who are able to sequence the main events of the Great Fire on their own. This time the five pictures showing the main events of the fire have been jumbled up. Ask them to cut them out carefully and rearrange them in the correct order on a fresh sheet of paper. They should then add sentences of their own describing the events shown in the pictures. A word bank is provided to help with spelling and vocabulary.

Activity sheet 3

This sheet is for more able children who can make their own decisions about the five most important events of the fire and place them in the correct sequence. The sheet provides only lines for writing on and a word bank. When the children have chosen the events and written about them, they should be encouraged to discuss the choices they made with friends. Get them to think carefully about how to move logically on from one step to another in their account, avoiding the use of the word 'then'. Discuss alternatives and look at the word bank, which provides a list of connectives to help them.

Plenary session

Share the responses to the activity sheets. Check how much the children remember about the main events of the fire and the order in which they happened. Use questions such as 'What happened before that?' and 'What happened next?'

Ideas for support

Where the activity sheets require cutting out and rearranging make sure the children check that their pictures are in the correct sequence before sticking them down. Support may be needed with cutting and sticking skills.

Provide class or individual word banks to help with writing tasks. Some assistance with words, especially place names is given on the activity sheets. Do provide help with grammar and punctuation in sentence writing, but paramount is the children's ability to read over their writing to check for its general sense.

Ideas for extension

Children could extend sequence activities to tell other stories in history, such as the Gunpowder Plot or the Spanish Armada. They could also place the main events they have covered in history in the correct sequence on a class timeline.

It will also help their appreciation of chronology and the passing of time if sequence activities are based on their own experiences. Possible activities might include how events happen in order during a typical day, the different events that happen each day during a week, the order of special events that take place in the school year. (See the timelining activities in Chapter 4.)

Linked ICT activities

Talk to the children about how a fire could start in their own homes and how we have to be careful not to cause one. Say we don't leave matches lying around, we don't leave candles lit in a room without being with them and don't leave things in front of a fire. Discuss ways of avoiding fire and what to do if they see one (i.e. how to contact the emergency services).

Tell the children that they are going to create a poster to warn people of the dangers of fire. Create the poster using a graphics program such as 'Dazzle', 'Fresco', Granada's 'Colours' or anything similar. Show the children how to use the line tool, the paintbrush tool and the shapes tool. Show them how to change the colour of these tools using the colour palette. Add some text to the picture, such as 'Always blow out your candles'. Print the posters and use them to raise awareness of fire around the school.

If possible ask someone from your local fire fighting team to come and judge the posters and to talk to the children about fire prevention.

What happened where?

Cut out the pictures and sentences about the Great Fire of London.
Match each sentence with a picture. Stick the picture and sentence together
on another sheet of paper in the order they happened.

The fire is nearly over.	The bridge falls down.
The fire starts in Pudding Lane.	The church is on fire.

Name _____

What happened where?

These pictures show important parts of the Great Fire of London. Cut them out and stick them in the correct order on a large sheet of paper. Under each picture, write a sentence to tell what it shows. Use the word bank to help you.

WORD BANK

Pudding Lane
Cheapside
St Paul's Cathedral
London Bridge
Pye Corner

PHOTOCOPIABLE

Name _____

What happened where?

Choose what you think are the five main parts of the story of the Great Fire of London. Write about them in the correct order. Use the word bank to help you. On the back of this sheet, draw which part of the story you think is the most important and say why.

1. _____

    _____

2. _____

    _____

3. _____

    _____

4. _____

    _____

5. _____

    _____

WORD BANK

at the start
after
next
during
the next day
soon afterwards
finally
at the end

2 *LESSON PLAN*

What happened next?

> **History objective**
> • To understand why the fire spread so far and stayed alight for so long.

Resources

- Newspaper pictures showing local fires
- Scenes of street life in seventeenth-century London
- Posters, pictures and literature on the fire service today
- Card, paper, scissors, glue, sentence cards for matching
- Generic sheets 1, 2 and 8 (pages 9, 10 and 16)
- Activity sheets 1–3 (pages 24–26)

Starting points: *whole class*

Briefly revise the details from the main story in the first lesson of how the fire started.

Ask the children to think about what happens when a large fire destroys buildings in a town. Talk about large fires they have seen on film, video and television news programmes. Discuss the possible causes of fires, such as matches, explosions and electrical faults. Talk about reasons why fires often spread rapidly, such as wind, dry weather, the presence of combustible materials like paper, card, fuel and rubber.

Discuss the methods and equipment used by modern fire-fighters in order to put fires out, such as water hoses, foam, turntable ladders and breathing apparatus. Use Generic sheet 2 to look at modern fire engines with the tools fire-fighters use and special devices like turntable ladders. Compare the battle against the fire in 1666 with the methods used today.

Use Generic sheet 1, along with other pictures, to show the children typical pictures of houses, churches and street scenes in London during the Stuart period. Discuss these scenes. Ask questions such as those on Generic sheet 8.

Talk about the effects of the fire, especially its spread and extent. Why did it spread so quickly in these streets? (See Generic sheet 8)

What would the children do if they were in the position of those people in London during the Great Fire? How would they try to escape? What would they take with them? What would they try to save?

Group activities

Activity sheet 1

This sheet, illustrated with a picture of the blaze, introduces children to some of the reasons why the Great Fire spread so rapidly and so far and why it stayed alight for such a long time. Children are given five sentences containing the connective 'because', which explain what happened during important stages of the fire. Key words have been missed out of these sentences and are given in a word bank. The children have to find the correct word to go into each space. Stress the importance of reading on to the end of the sentence in order to make a better guess at what the missing word is.

Activity sheet 2

On this sheet the children are required to give reasons for the severity of the fire. Six 'broken' sentences are given on the sheet. Children will need to cut out the twelve strips and match them up to form completed sentences about the fire, such as 'The fire went out because … the wind died down'. Illustrations are given on the sheet in order to help them, such as people sheltering in churches because they were made from stone. Before they start work on the sheet discuss with the children the importance of the connective 'because' as the link word in sentences that explain, especially in history, why certain events happened.

Activity sheet 3

This sheet is aimed at more able children who can construct their own sentences about why the Great Fire of London spread so quickly and why it stayed alight for the best part of six days. This time the opening part of eight sentences is given and the children are expected to complete the sentence themselves. As an additional task they should make their own sentences, including those about what happened after the fire. Again, discuss with them the importance of the word 'because' in these sentences as a lead in to the explanation of events.

Plenary session

Reinforce the main purpose of the lesson by playing a 'runaround' matching game. Take five or six of the broken sentences used on the activity sheets and write them in large letters with a marker pen on pieces of card. Give a piece of card each to ten or twelve children in the class. Invite them to the front of the class. Get them to find their partner by matching up the correct parts of the sentence. An example might be: 'People escaped to churches…' goes with '…because they were made of stone'. Set a time limit, perhaps ten or twenty seconds. Repeat with other groups of children. When the matching has been done, read the sentences aloud and then pin the cards onto a more permanent wall display.

Ideas for support

Prepare the children with plenty of sentence construction work. Give them the beginning of sentences and ask them to complete them or give endings and ask for suitable beginnings. Work on conjunctions and the useful part they play in linking ideas in a sentence. Look particularly at the word 'because' as a conjunction that links a fact with an explanation in a sentence. Give examples of this word in sentences related to the children themselves: 'We cannot go out to play because it is raining,' or 'We need to change now because it is time for PE.'

Ideas for extension

Discuss the event in terms of cause and effect and the important role it plays in history.

Compare and contrast life now and life in seventeenth-century London. How have things stayed the same? How have they changed?

Look at the changes that have taken place in methods of fire fighting. Find out more about today's fire fighting services by inviting a representative to visit the school to answer questions or arrange a visit to the local fire station. Discuss aspects of fire safety as it applies to our own homes today. What advice does the fire service give?

Linked ICT activities

Use the internet to find sites that provide information about the fire services in your area and what they do to help the public to keep safe from fires. Using any word processing program that will allow you to create a word bank, such as 'Talking Write Away', 'Textease' or 'Clicker 4', create a word bank with words that will help the children to describe what the fire service does. Ask the children to use the words in the word bank to describe the job of the fire-fighter. You may find your local fire service will be happy to pay the school a visit to talk to them about fire prevention.

Talk to the children about how the fire started in London. Could a fire start like that today? If it did would it spread as fast? How do we stop fires from spreading? Using the word processing program ask the children to make a list (working in small groups of four or five) of all the different ways that we would stop a fire from spreading today.

Name _____

What happened next?

Look carefully at the picture of the Great Fire of London.
Complete the sentences. Use the words in the word bank to help you.

The fire started because the _____ did not put his ovens out when he went to bed.

The fire spread quickly because of a strong _____.

Most people ran away because they were very _____.

People ran to churches because they were made of _____.

The fire went out because the wind _____.

WORD BANK

stopped   stone   baker   wind   scared

PHOTOCOPIABLE

Name _____

What happened next?

Cut out the text boxes and match them to make sentences that
tell what happened during the Great Fire of London.
Use the pictures to help you.

The blaze started because	they thought water would be safe.
The fire spread quickly because	they were very scared.
Most people ran away because	they were made of stone.
Some ran to churches because	a baker did not put his fires out.
Some went onto the river because	the wind died down.
The fire went out because	it was dry and very windy.

Name _____

What happened next?

Complete the sentences given below. Think carefully.

1. The blaze started in a baker's shop in Pudding Lane because

    _____

2. The fire spread very quickly to other houses and shops because

    _____

3. The flames had plenty of fuel to help them because

    _____

4. Most people left their homes and ran away because

    _____

5. Some people escaped to shelter in churches because

    _____

6. Others got into boats and rowed to the centre of the River Thames
    because

    _____

7. The fire finally went out after four or five days because

    _____

8. The fire lasted for such a long time because

    _____

Now think up your own sentences.
What new homes were built after the fire?
What were they like?
Write your sentences on the back of this sheet.

PHOTOCOPIABLE

Eyewitness accounts

History objective
• To understand how we know about the Great Fire.

Resources

• Newspaper accounts of fires
• Word banks
• Generic sheets 1, 3, 4, 6 and 8 (pages 9, 11, 12, 14 and 16)
• Activity sheets 1–3 (pages 29–31)

Starting points: *whole class*

Show the children newspaper accounts of recent events, preferably local, that give details of disasters like fires and floods. Discuss the general layout that newspapers use, such as large pictures showing scenes from the event, the use of bold headlines to attract readers and written details of the event set down in columns of print.

Ask if anyone knows what an eyewitness account is. Why do newspapers find them so valuable? Discuss organisations that find eyewitnesses very useful, such as the police when they are investigating a crime or a road accident. Talk about the fact that different witnesses do not always see events in the same way.

Explain to the children that one of the reasons why we know so much about the Great Fire of London is because a number of detailed yet different eyewitness accounts were written.

Tell them about the people who wrote these accounts, such as Samuel Pepys, John Evelyn, the Earl of Clarendon and Sir Thomas Bludworth. Show them the portraits of these characters on Generic sheet 4. Talk about their appearance and what they are wearing. Read short extracts from some of the accounts they wrote (see Generic sheet 3). Point out that we have also learned much about the fire from details written by ordinary people like the 15-year-old boy, William Taswell, mentioned on Generic sheet 3.

Tell the children they are going to write diary accounts of events during the Great Fire of London. Explain that there was no television, radio or film then and that these accounts would be the only real record of what actually happened. Their eyewitness accounts should focus on what they would be able to see, hear and smell. Invite them to close their eyes and 'visualise' the scene. What do they see, hear, smell and feel now? Share words from Generic sheet 6.

Group activities

Activity sheet 1

This sheet is aimed at children who may need a specific character to help them focus on the scenes that would have been witnessed in London when the Great Fire was at its height. A picture of the character in seventeenth-century costume is provided along with a blank page from the diary for them to fill in. They should write short sentences using as much detailed description as they possibly can. Emphasise that although the sentences are short, each one should be completely different. A word bank is provided on the sheet.

Activity sheet 2

This sheet provides two blank pages from Samuel Pepys' diary for Monday 3 September and Tuesday 4 September 1666 when the fire would have been at its worst. Using the word bank on Generic sheet 6 the children should write colourful accounts of aspects of the fire for both of the days in the first person as if they were actually there. They should look carefully at the diary extracts provided (Generic sheet 3). They are then asked to help keep a class diary during a typical week in as much detail as possible. They could take it in turns to do a day each. They should try to include some eyewitness accounts of when they have been present when something has happened.

Activity sheet 3

This sheet is aimed at more able children and gives them greater independence when they are writing diary entries about the Great Fire of London in the style of Samuel Pepys. They are given blank diary pages for the main four days that the fire was raging and are asked to write their own detailed account of what eyewitnesses would have seen, heard and smelt. These children should look more closely at the diary extracts of Pepys and Evelyn on Generic sheet 3 to get a better idea of the style that was used. Through discussion, give help in transforming the language conventions of seventeenth-century England into our own language today. Encourage good use of vocabulary, especially appropriate verbs and colourful adjectives. Let them use Generic sheet 6.

The final task on this sheet is to make a diary entry about what will happen after the fire. This can focus on some of the rebuilding plans.

Plenary session

Select examples of work from each of the three activity groups and mount a classroom display of the finished work. Discuss the way in which children have written the first-hand diary accounts. How have they captured how people must have felt in London at that time?

Revise key issues raised during the session. How do we know so much about the Great Fire? Who were Samuel Pepys and John Evelyn? Why did their diaries turn out to be so important? What did they tell us that we did not know already?

Ideas for support

Provide plenty of visual stimulation to help with first-hand eyewitness accounts of the fire. Provide individual or class word banks to assist with vocabulary. Stress that the events the children write about should contain as much variety as possible. For example, what happened to buildings, how the people of London reacted, and how some tried to fight the fire as best as they could.

Emphasise the importance of good punctuation in the accounts and also neat handwriting and general presentation to make the diary accounts appealing.

Ideas for extension

Talk about the contribution that diaries can make in finding out about what happened in the past. Do the children or any of their family keep a diary? If they kept a diary what sort of things would they record in it? How useful would the diary be? If this was read by people in the future, what would it tell them about life today?

Tell the children that Pepys recorded in his diary what he did with his most precious possessions like money and silver and also wine and cheese. He moved some out of London for safety and buried others in pits in the ground. What valued items would the children choose to save if their house was threatened by fire and why? Can they think of other ways of keeping their valuable possessions safe?

Look at extracts from Pepys' diary that explain what happened in London once the fire had gone out and people began to return to their homes. Investigate the various rebuilding plans that were put forward. How successful were they? Find out more about the life and work of the architect–builder Sir Christopher Wren and the work he did on the rebuilding of London.

Linked ICT activities

Tell the children they are going to imagine what it would have been like living in Pudding Lane at the time of the Great Fire. They are going to record on a tape recorder their own diary of the day that the fire broke out from the time that they found out about the fire to the time when they had to leave London to get away from the fire. First discuss some of the things that may have happened to them, such as having to rescue some family or friends. They may have been trapped and had to find a way out. Say that they should pretend to be a character and give them a card with the name of the person and how old they are. Let them work in groups with a classroom assistant or parent helper to record their diary. Let them use the tape recorder so that they can stop and start it when they may need to. Use the tape recordings as part of a listening activity or a starting point for writing the diary. It may also be used during circle time to discuss with the children aspects of PHSE on helping each other.

Name _____

Eyewitness

This boy kept a diary about the Great Fire of London.
What did he see, hear and smell? Fill in the diary page.

My diary by _____

WORD BANK

saw   buckets   people   started   water   fire   flames
burning   smoke   wood   house   shouting   crying   running

Name _____

Eyewitness

You are Samuel Pepys. Write in your diary what you see, hear and smell during the Great Fire of London. Use the two diary pages below and the word bank on Generic sheet 6.

Monday 3 September 1666

Tuesday 4 September 1666

Think of some things you could write in a class diary. Talk about them with some of your friends.

PHOTOCOPIABLE

Eyewitness

You are Samuel Pepys, the famous diary writer. What do you see, hear and smell as you go around London during the Great Fire? How does it make you feel? Use the blank diary pages below to write your own account.

Sunday 2 September	Monday 3 September

Tuesday 4 September	Wednesday 5 September

Make other entries in the diary on the back of the sheet. For example, what happened after the fire?

CHAPTER 2

The Olympic Games

Background

Unlike most of the other important ancient civilisations, Greece was never a united country. The people who inhabited these lands (see the map on Generic sheet 2) called themselves Greeks, spoke a common language and followed much the same customs, but they actually belonged to a group of powerful city-states such as Athens and Sparta, each with its own government, army and system of trade.

The Minoan civilisation began as early as 3200BC on the island of Crete and the city of Mycenae grew to prominence on the Greek mainland around 1600BC. But the truly 'golden age' of Ancient Greece came with the emergence of the city-states. They lasted from around 800BC to 146BC when mainland Greece became a Roman province. It was also during this period that more Greeks began to leave the mainland to settle on nearby islands and the Greek influence also spread to other regions within the Mediterranean, such as North Africa, Asia Minor (Turkey) and parts of southern Italy where Greek colonies were set up.

Life in the villages and cities of Ancient Greece was very structured. The wealthy few lived in luxury. This gave them the opportunity to study, take exercise, visit the theatre and become involved in local politics. Most of the population, however, were poor and had to work hard to earn a living. The way in which society was organised allowed free-born Greek men to have a say in the way their city-state was run, but women and foreigners were treated as second-class citizens, and slaves, many of whom had been captured in war, faced a harsh existence. Democracy extended to men over 18 who had been born in the city or the surrounding area. They could vote on issues including electing officials and declaring war and peace. Women, slaves and foreigners had no vote. In Athens every citizen had the right to speak at the assembly that was held on a hill called the Pnyx about every ten days. As many as 6,000 men could attend and if numbers were low police visited the city rounding up extra people.

There was no organised education system as such, although boys from wealthy families were expected to attend school between the ages of seven and 18. Instruction could take place at the home of the teacher while some tutors travelled around the cities and carried out lessons in the open air. The curriculum consisted mainly of reading, writing, counting, music and physical activity such as gymnastics. Learning to speak in public and the ability to recite long passages of poetry were also thought to be important. In some city-states, such as Sparta, boys left school early to begin training as soldiers.

On rare occasions girls were taught reading and writing by tutors at home, but generally they were expected to help their mothers in the house and learn skills such as spinning and weaving. For children there was some time for playing with toys like dolls, soldiers and board games, but childhood was short. By the age of 12 boys had often left home for army training and girls were usually married. Greek families were usually large but child mortality was high and only about half of the children born could expect to reach the age of 20.

Partly because much of the rocky barren land in Greece was so difficult to cultivate, the Greeks became the greatest traders of their time. Sea travel was always the easiest and most popular form of getting around the mainland and islands of Ancient Greece. This made the Greeks natural sailors and, with the sea acting as their link to faraway places, Greek traders were able to travel to other regions in the Mediterranean and beyond. The Greeks sold commodities such as wine, olive oil and pottery abroad and imported items that they could not produce enough of themselves, such as copper (from Spain), grain (Cyprus, Italy and Sicily), ivory (North Africa), textiles (Egypt) and timber (Italy).

Although the inhabitants of the Greek city-states had much in common there was a fierce rivalry between them. Quarrels and wars between them were frequent and they seem almost to have taken it in turns to be the most dominant. There were no permanent armies, except in the case of Sparta, and when war was declared it was the duty of every male citizen to enlist. Once hostilities had ceased, those who survived usually returned to their normal work. Only on rare occasions did these diverse city-states join forces to fight a common enemy. They united for the Trojan wars towards the end of the twelfth century BC, the war against the Persians in the sixth and fifth centuries BC and under the command of Alexander the Great in the fourth century BC. While the first two events were intended to ward off invasion, the third was to bring about Alexander's ambition to extend the Greek Empire as far as he could.

We know much about everyday life in Ancient Greece and some of the main events that occurred in its history because there were many Greek writers who made records at the time. Archaeologists who have excavated Greek towns and cities over the years have found many objects, including pots often decorated with scenes from everyday life.

The origins of the Olympic Games

The organisation of large-scale sporting events grew out of the Greeks' belief that a healthy mind needed to be combined with a healthy body. The events also played an important role in religious festivals and were seen as a way for people to honour the gods.

The four most important events were the Pythian, the Nemean, the Isthmian and the Olympic Games and they were open to competitors from all the Greek city-states, regions and colonies. Although the Olympic Games started as a small gathering, it gradually grew larger and more popular until it became the leading event. The Games usually lasted for five days although athletes would have been in training for months beforehand. There were several days of religious activities followed by three days of events. The Games always ended with a celebration banquet in honour of the winners who were rewarded with ribbons, garlands of leaves or wreaths.

The first record of the Olympic Games dates from 776BC when an individual named Coroebus from Elis, a cook, won the prestigious sprint contest. However, the event probably started at least 500 years before this. Held every four years, the Games ran continuously for almost 1,000 years. They became so important that wars were halted by a sacred truce while the Games were being held and

the progress of Greek history was recorded according to the Olympiad – the four-year period in which the Games took place. The event was stopped in AD393 on the orders of the Roman Emperor Theodosius, probably because of its connection with pagan worship.

The ancient Olympic Games, held in honour of the ruler of the gods, Zeus, takes its name from a place called Olympia located in the region of Greece known now as western Peloponnese. According to Greek legend, a thunderbolt released by Zeus landed here so he claimed the land as sacred ground. Excavations started in 1829 concentrated on the Temple of Zeus and by the early 1960s much of the area had been restored. Among many other things, the museum at Olympia houses the largest collections of Ancient Greek weapons in the world. Excavations on the site uncovered hostels, baths and other accommodation for the large number of visitors who attended the Games.

The most important events of the Games – the running races – were held on a straight, flat track surrounded by a sloping embankment of earth for the spectators. The track was about 192 metres long (one *stade*) and 32 metres wide and had space for about 20 runners at a time. The starting line was a row of stones embedded in the track. Grooves were cut in the stone to give the athletes a better grip. Longer running races were the *diaulos* (two *stades*) and the *dolichos*, which varied, but might go up to 24 *stades*.

There were also throwing competitions, with discus and javelin, and the long jump in which the competitors carried weights in each hand to help them go further. Boxing and wrestling were also included and a combination of the two called *pankration* in which almost anything was allowed apart from biting, breaking fingers and eye gouging. Sometimes soldiers (*hoplites*) competed in races wearing helmets and greaves (leg guards) and carrying shields.

Horse and chariot racing took place in the nearby hippodrome. In the pentathlon, athletes took part in discus and javelin throwing, jumping, running and wrestling all in the same day. Women were never allowed at the Olympic Games even as spectators, but in some areas, such as Sparta, they did have their own separate games.

The modern Olympic Games

The Games were revived in 1894 largely as the brainchild of a French nobleman called Baron Pierre de Coubertin who suggested the idea at an international sports conference in Paris. The International Olympic Committee (IOC) was formed and the first games were held in Athens in honour of the Greeks in 1896. Pierre de Coubertin became the first President of the Committee and hoped that international sporting competitions would help the different countries of the world to get on better with each other. Thirteen countries were represented, there were about 300 competitors, and the 42 events covered ten different sports.

When the new Games were launched, de Coubertin expressed the views held long ago by the athletes of Ancient Greece. He said, 'The most important thing in the Games is not to win but to take part, just as the most important thing in life is not the triumph but the struggle. The essential thing is not to have conquered but to have fought well.'

One of the races in the 1896 Games was run from the plains of Marathon, north of Athens to the new stadium. It marked the journey made in 490BC by the messenger Pheidippides who ran from the battlefield at Marathon to announce the news of the Athenian victory over the Persians before dropping dead. Appropriately, this first marathon race, a distance of about 42 kilometres, was won by the Greek athlete, Spyridon Louis.

There are many traditions associated with the Olympic Games today. A sacred flame is carried around the world from Olympia and lit in the city holding the Games. The Olympic flag has rings to indicate the five continents of the world and includes at least one colour from the flag of every country taking part. Competitors and officials live together in a large village while the Games are in progress. The motto of the Olympic Games is 'Citius (Faster), Altius (Higher) and Fortius (Stronger).' The Greek team always leads the procession at the opening ceremony while the host nation always comes last. The Olympic oath is spoken by one athlete at the opening ceremony of every Games:

'In the name of all the competitors, I promise that we shall take part in these Olympic Games, respecting and abiding by the rules which govern them, in the true spirit of sportsmanship, for the glory of sport, and the honour of our teams.'

In the 1996 Games in Atlanta, USA, over 10,000 people from almost 200 countries took part in 271 different medal events making it the world's largest sporting event. The Games continue to be held on a four-year cycle. There are World Paralympic Games for disabled competitors and these are usually held later in the same cities as the Olympic Games. The Winter Olympic Games, established in 1924, is mainly for sports carried out on snow and ice, so it is held in different venues from the Olympic Games.

There is a monument to Pierre de Coubertin at Olympia, and when he died in 1937 his heart was buried there.

Note: The children will need an explanation to help them understand the difference between BC (Before Christ) and AD (anno domini – in the year of our Lord). Some sources now use BCE (Before the Common Era) instead of BC.

Europe

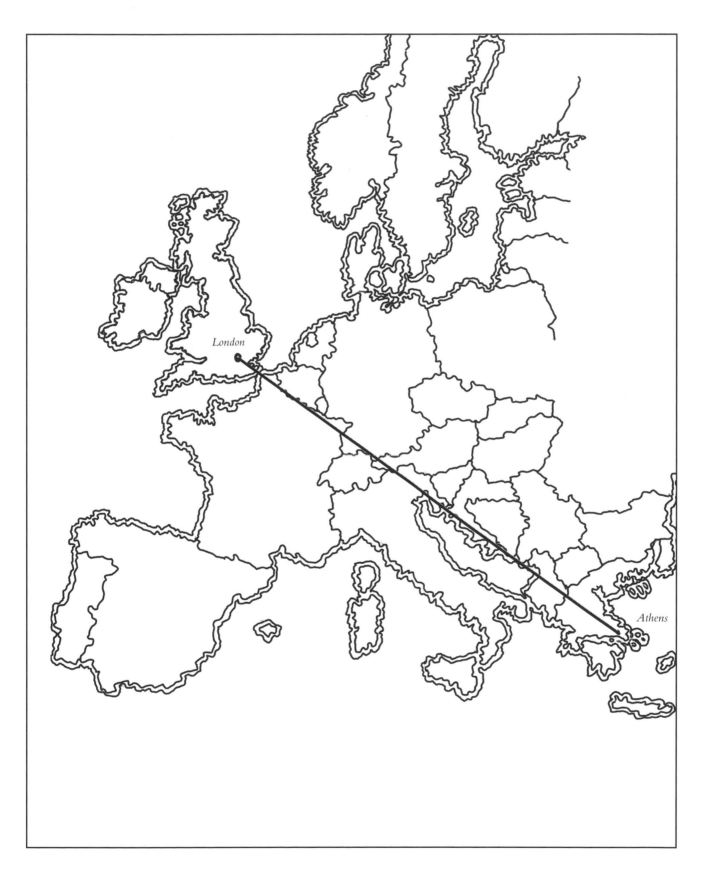

Ancient Greece

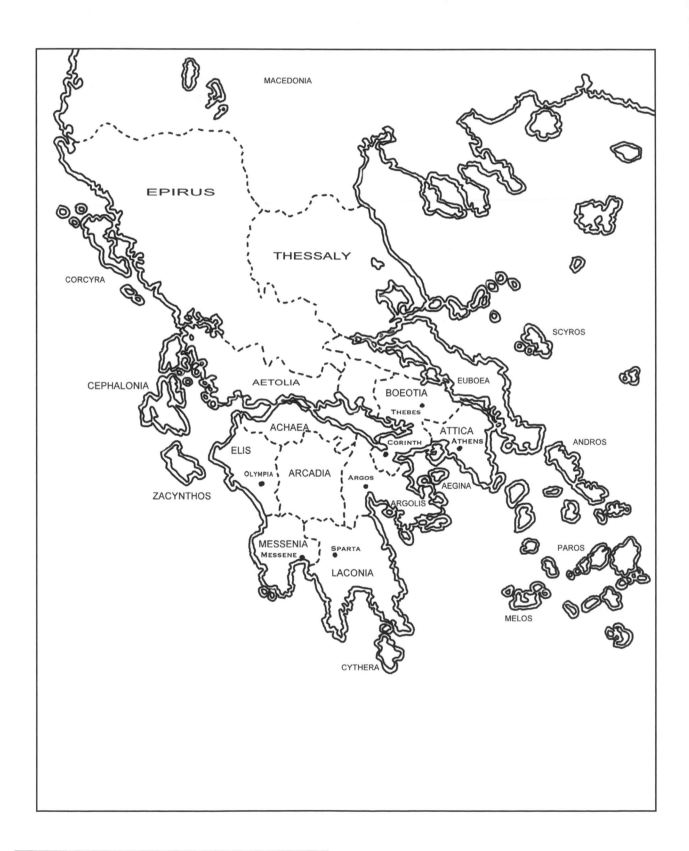

MACEDONIA

EPIRUS

THESSALY

CORCYRA

CEPHALONIA

AETOLIA

BOEOTIA

Thebes

SCYROS

EUBOEA

ATTICA

Athens

ANDROS

ACHAEA

Corinth

ELIS

OLYMPIA

ARCADIA

Argos

AEGINA

ZACYNTHOS

ARGOLIS

PAROS

MESSENIA

Messene

Sparta

LACONIA

MELOS

CYTHERA

A timeline

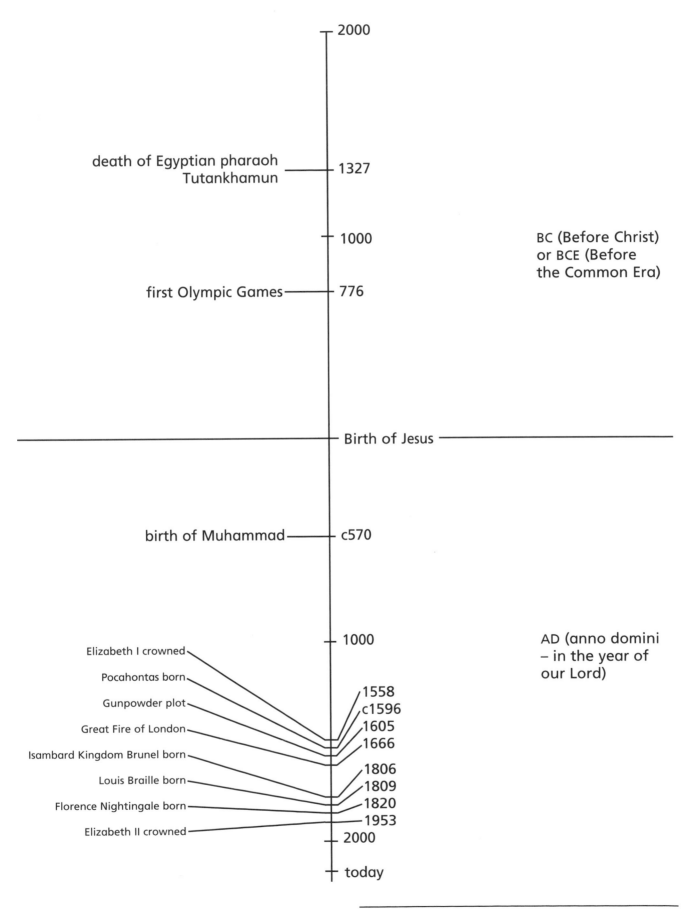

2000

death of Egyptian pharaoh
Tutankhamun —— 1327

1000   BC (Before Christ)
                             or BCE (Before
first Olympic Games —— 776   the Common Era)

——————— Birth of Jesus ———————

birth of Muhammad —— c570

1000   AD (anno domini
                             – in the year of
                             our Lord)

Elizabeth I crowned ——— 1558
Pocahontas born ——— c1596
Gunpowder plot ——— 1605
Great Fire of London ——— 1666
Isambard Kingdom Brunel born ——— 1806
Louis Braille born ——— 1809
Florence Nightingale born ——— 1820
                         ——— 1953
Elizabeth II crowned ——— 2000

today

Life in Ancient Greece

The Olympic Games

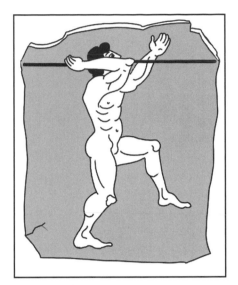  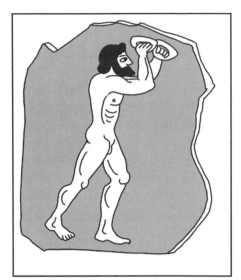

  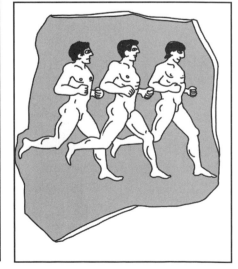

The Games today

Questions and answers

- **What sort of houses did they live in?** Poorer families lived in small single-storey houses with all the rooms enclosed. Those with more money would have larger buildings with more rooms arranged around a central courtyard.

- **What were the houses made from?** Stone was used for the foundations of a house with the walls being made from mud bricks dried in the sun. The roof was made from pottery tiles. Windows were small and high up on walls. Floors were usually beaten earth covered with rugs and furniture was limited to chairs, tables, beds and storage baskets and boxes.

- **Did the Ancient Greeks have families like ours?** Families were generally large. Parents, children and other relatives such as grandparents, aunts, uncles and cousins might live together in the same house. Married women were usually much younger than their husbands. Some were married around the age of 12. They stayed at home most of the time looking after the children, cooking and taking care of the house.

- **Did children go to school?** In most places only boys from wealthy families did. They were taught reading, writing, public speaking and some music. There was also physical exercise. In Sparta, boys left school early to train as soldiers in the army. Girls stayed at home and may have learned to read and write there. They were also taught how to run the household.

- **What sort of games did they play?** They played with painted clay dolls and babies had clay rattles. They enjoyed ball games and had hoops and spinning tops. They played board games like draughts. When they were 12, children were expected to stop playing with toys to show they had left childhood behind.

- **What happened if they were ill?** Some asked the god of medicine and healing, Asclepius, to make them better. But some doctors, such as Hippocrates, examined patients and looked carefully for symptoms. Then they prescribed a cure, often a herbal remedy, combined with good diet and exercise.

- **Who went to work?** Most people, unless they were very wealthy, had to go to work. The rich had slaves to work for them.

- **What sort of jobs did they have?** In the countryside most people farmed the land. In towns there would be many trade and craft workers like bakers, potters, jewellers, weavers and carpenters. Towns would also have lawyers, teachers and doctors.

- **Where did families get their food?** Most food was grown on farms locally and brought in to the local market despite the fact that Greece tended to have poor soil. Extra food supplies like grain were imported from nearby countries.

- **What sort of food did they eat?** Meat was rare unless people hunted for it themselves. Fish were plentiful. Bread and cheese were eaten. There were plenty of fruits like olives, figs, dates, grapes, apples and pears and vegetables like peas, beans, cabbage and carrots. Most people drank wine mixed with water.

- **What sort of clothes did they wear?** Outfits were loose and light to keep the wearers cool. They were made of fine wool or linen and fixed with pins and brooches. Men, women and children wore similar garments. The main garment was the tunic (chiton) and a cloak (himation). Belts were tied around the waist and leather sandals worn on the feet.

- **How did people travel around?** Roads were often no better than dusty tracks. Journeys across country were on foot or by donkey. For longer journeys they used horse-drawn carriages. If the journey could be made by sea that is how people preferred to travel.

Questions and answers

- **Why did the Ancient Greeks hold Games?** There were three main reasons. Greek life revolved around religion and sport was a way of showing respect to and worshipping the gods. Men had to keep themselves fit in case they needed to fight. The Greeks believed they should have a healthy mind and a healthy body.

- **Why did they become so important?** Because it gave the opportunity for the different city-states to meet together in friendly competition. As time progressed, however, they became over competitive and some city-states used the Games to show their rivals just how strong they were. Winning at the Games became very much a status symbol.

- **How do we know they were important?** Any wars that were being fought at the time were suspended by a sacred truce until the Games were over. People were given time to get back home after the Games before hostilities started again. The Greeks recorded historical events according to the 'Olympiad', the four-year period in which the Games took place.

- **Where were the games first held?** There were many local games festivals but the most important in Greece were the Pythian Games at Delphi, the Isthmian Games at Corinth, the Nemean Games at Nemea and the Olympic Games at Olympia. The first recorded Games at Olympia were in 776BC, but they probably started hundreds of years before this.

- **How often did they take place?** The Olympic Games were held every four years and were in honour of the Greeks' chief god Zeus. They always took place between early August and mid September.

- **Who took part in the Games?** The best athletes from the 100 or so city-states in Greece would take part in the Games. They trained for much of the rest of the year to get ready for the Games and brought their trainers with them to Olympia. Women could not take part, although there were a few city-states such as Sparta who held separate games for women.

- **Who came to watch them?** Spectators from all the city-states would follow their athletes to support them. Olympia was not a town in itself but just the site used for the games. It provided accommodation for the spectators. Women and girls were banned from watching and could be punished if they were

caught doing so. Food, flowers and other goods were on sale and musicians, singers and dancers also kept the crowds entertained.

- **What events did they have?** Running races over different lengths of the track and a hoplite race for soldiers in armour. Hoplite was the name given to infantry or foot soldiers in Greek armies. Throwing events involved the discus and javelin. There was a long jump event, wrestling and boxing and penkration, a combination of both these two. The pentathlon included five different events – running, wrestling, long jump, javelin and discus. There was horse racing and chariot racing.

- **What facilities did they use?** Running races, throwing and jumping events took place in the stadium. Chariot and horse racing were held in the hippodrome. The judges sat in a special box, but spectators were expected to stand. Training areas were provided for the athletes. Olympia had an open-air swimming pool but it is unlikely to have been used for competitions.

- **How were the winners rewarded?** They were awarded prizes: garlands or wreaths made out of laurel, olive or pine; or sometimes it might be a statue or a victory ode or poem. They were treated as heroes when they arrived back home. Some athletes became professional and were paid wages to compete by their home city-state.

- **How long did the games last?** Five days. The games always opened with a religious ceremony in which competitors and judges promised to keep to the rules. Then the events began. There was a break halfway through for another religious ceremony. At the end of the events prizes were awarded and there was a final banquet before people set off home.

- **When and why did they eventually stop?** No records of the Olympic Games are given after AD261 but it is not certain when they came to an end. When Greece became part of the Roman Empire pagan ceremonies were banned. In AD426 the Roman Emperor Theodosius had the temple of Zeus and other buildings at Olympia burned down and after that the site was abandoned until discovered by archaeologists many centuries later.

Questions and answers

- **How important are the Games now?** They are rightly regarded as the largest sporting event now held in the world. More than 10,000 competitors from some 200 countries take part and some 15,000 journalists send reports all over the world. Television audiences top the 3.5 billion mark. Acting as host to the Games is a major undertaking involving organising the competitions, arranging transport and looking after the security of thousands of people.

- **Why are they still so important?** Athletes in the various sports regard the Olympic Games as the premier event they can take part in. Winning an Olympic gold medal is still thought to be the highest achievement of a person's sporting career. The Games also provide work opportunities for many people, especially since 1984 when host cities were allowed to use advertising and sponsorship to help meet costs.

- **How often do the modern Games take place?** The main Summer Games are still held every four years. Since 1992 the Winter Games, with events based on ice and snow, have taken place on their own four-year cycle. World Paralympic Games for disabled competitors are usually held later in the same cities as the Olympic Games.

- **Who takes part in the Games now?** Whereas the first of the revived Olympic Games in Athens in 1896 was open to anyone who wanted to attend, the Games today are only intended for the top athletes from each of the competing countries. Athletes have to reach a certain qualifying standard before they are allowed to take part.

- **Who comes to watch them?** Because of the ease of travel, people are able to attend the Olympic Games from many parts of the world. Attendance figures at the Sydney Olympics in 2000 were estimated at around five million. The launching of satellites in space now means events can be shown as they happen all around the world.

- **What events do they have?** Only ten different sports were included in the 1896 Games in Athens, but new ones have been added at almost every Games since then. Some sports have been dropped including rugby, cricket and polo with the current list standing at a total of 28, ranging from archery to wrestling and from handball to triathlon. Athletics, gymnastics and aquatics (such as swimming and diving) usually attract most spectators.

- **What facilities do they use?** The city hosting the Summer Games usually builds a large new stadium. This is used for the opening and closing ceremonies and also for most of the athletics events. Other venues have to be found for sports like swimming, boxing, cycling and football. The Sydney Olympic Stadium had a capacity of 110,000 although this was cut by 30,000 after the Games so it could be used for events like large rugby matches. Since 1932 most of the competitors have lived in a specially constructed Olympic Village, which reverts to ordinary housing once the Games are finished.

- **How are the winners rewarded?** Winners in Athens in 1896 were presented with a silver medal, an olive branch and a certificate. The runners–up received a copper medal and a sprig of laurel. Today, winners receive a gold medal, those in second place a silver medal, and the third placed competitor a bronze medal. Fourth to eighth places receive a diploma. The last solid gold medals for winners were awarded in 1912. Now the winner's 'gold' medal is actually silver gilt although it does contain about six grams of fine gold. Medals awarded in the Paralympics also have inscriptions written in Braille.

- **How long do the games last?** This depends on the seasonal climate conditions of the host country, but they are usually in late summer or early autumn. The Sydney Olympics lasted from 15 September until 1 October – a period of 17 days.

- **What traditions from the past have remained unchanged?** The swearing of the Olympic oath, the torch relay that carries the sacred flame from Olympia to the city staging the Games, and the five-ringed Olympic flag. Doves of peace are always released from cages at the opening ceremony. It is also a tradition that the Greek team always leads out the competitors at the opening ceremony and that the team of the host nation always goes last.

- **What plans are there for the future of the Games?** It is difficult to predict. Venues are decided up to seven years in advance but no one knows who will be taking part, what new events may be added, or what records will be broken. Whatever happens, athletes will always be reminded that the most important thing is 'not to win but to take part'.

The Olympic Games

1
LESSON PLAN

Resources

- Maps of Europe and Greece
- Holiday souvenirs and photographs, postcards, travel brochures
- Visual information showing everyday life in Ancient Greece including housing, clothing, education, games, travel, occupations etc
- Large class timeline (BC to AD)
- Generic sheets 1–4 and 7 (pages 35–38 and 41)
- Activity sheets 1–3 (pages 46–48)

Starting points: *whole class*

The purpose of this lesson is to help children find out more about what life was like for people living in Ancient Greece over 2,000 years ago and also to make comparisons between life then and life now. It features the topics that would have most affected ordinary people, especially children, such as housing, clothing, food, education and leisure.

Display a large map of Europe in the classroom several days before the lesson, with Britain and Greece clearly labelled. (You could use Generic sheet 1, which also shows the route from Britain to Greece. Enlarge it and label the two countries.) Alongside it display the map of Ancient Greece (Generic sheet 2). Support these maps with posters, holiday souvenirs, postcards and cuttings from travel brochures about the country.

Ask the children if any of them have been on holiday to Greece. What do they remember about the scenery, the buildings, the weather and the food? Why do they think Greece and its islands are a popular place for people to visit on their holidays? Some may have photographs of a holiday in Greece that they can bring into school. Use Generic sheet 2 to look at the different locations such as mainland Greece and some of its main islands: Corfu, Crete, Rhodes and Zante.

Tell the children that they are going to find out what it was like to live in Greece some 2,500 years ago. Stress that this period of time is usually referred to in history as Ancient Greece. Discuss what the word 'ancient' means. Use the timeline on Generic sheet 3 to demonstrate how long ago this period of time was (a difficult concept for younger children). Compare how long ago it was with other events and the lives of people in history, such as the Great Fire of London, the Gunpowder Plot, the coronation of Queen Elizabeth II. With reference to the timeline and other events on it, explain the meaning of BC, AD and BCE. Show the children that the dates connected to Ancient Greece come in the BC and BCE section.

Point to the map of Ancient Greece and explain that in those days the area was made up of city-states, which were often enemies with each other but also joined together to fight common enemies. Say that today, the country is united and there are no such internal battles.

Explain to the children that we know so much about what life was like for the Ancient Greeks because of the items that have been left behind. Evidence has come not only through archaeologists who have dug up temples, stadiums, statues, sculpture and other artefacts but also from wall paintings and everyday objects such as vases. These show pictures of ordinary people carrying out routine tasks such as reading and writing, farming, being craft-workers, playing instruments, dancing and enjoying games. Show them pictures and photographs of examples of these objects and activities (see Generic sheet 4). How many of these things are done by people today? List them on the board. Explain that there were many important writers working in Ancient Greece and that some of the things they have written, especially about battles and wars and the heroes who appear in stories and legends, have remained for us to read.

Then, using the visual resources and directed questions (see Generic sheet 7), discuss how people lived in Ancient Greece over 2,000 years ago.

Group activities

These can be used with children individually or with them working in pairs or small groups.

Activity sheet 1

This sheet is intended for children who will need support to recognise visual information about the kind of everyday tasks and activities people had to carry out in Ancient Greece. They are required to match captions to the scenes depicted on the pottery shown. It may be necessary to discuss the pictures with them first.

Activity sheet 2

In this activity the children have to complete the captions to the pictures of ancient Greek pottery showing everyday scenes from Ancient Greek life.

Activity sheet 3

This sheet is for more able children who should be able to write whole captions describing what is on the pottery and draw one piece of pottery in the style of the Ancient Greeks to show what is written in the caption.

Plenary session

Sit in the 'hot seat' and become a citizen of Ancient Greece. Let the children ask you questions about your life. You could hold an artefact to base the interview on. Where was it bought? Who made it? What is it used for? Extend this to include other questions about life in those times. In time children may be able to take over in the 'hot seat' and answer the questions themselves.

Ideas for support

Plenty of visual resources will be needed if children are to derive maximum benefit from these activities. Focus strongly on timelining tasks so that children begin to appreciate how long ago the civilisation existed in Ancient Greece. Provide well-labelled maps of Europe in general and Greece in particular to assist children with location work. Help may be needed finding and using book resources from the history section of the Key Stage 1 library.

Ideas for extension

Design and technology sessions can be used to make actual models of Greek pottery from clay. These can be decorated with scenes from everyday life. Children can research and find out more about aspects of life in Ancient Greece which have not been covered, such as Greek gods and the life of Alexander the Great. Contrasts can be made between the lifestyles of people living in different city-states, especially Athens and Sparta. Groups of children can create a tableau of the scenes shown on the side of Greek pots. Other groups have to guess what activity the children are representing.

Linked ICT activities

Using the Greek pottery as a starting point, discuss with the children the types of geometric designs and the patterns on the pottery created using straight lines. Tell them that they are going to create a design for a special Greek pot which could have been used to commemorate the Olympic Games. They must use ideas from the patterns and designs they have been looking at on the Greek pots. Using a graphics program such as Granada's 'Colours', 'Fresco', 'Dazzle' or anything similar, create a black background on the screen as a starting point by filling the screen black. Show the children how to use the line tool, paintbrush and shapes tool. Using these tools ask them to select colours used on the Greek pots to create their own pattern and design for their pot. Print out the final design and, using different card templates of Greek pots, ask the children to choose a style of pot and to cut their design out into the style of the pot.

Pottery

Look at these Ancient Greek vases. Match what is on them to the captions below.

Here are people gathering olives from a tree.	Here are some men playing musical instruments.
This is a child playing on a hobby horse.	Here are some ladies carrying water from the local fountain.

Name _____

Pottery

Look at these Ancient Greek vases. Complete the captions.

Here are _____

olives from _____

Here are _____

_____

This is a _____

on a hobby horse.

Here are some _____

_____ water jars.

Name _____

Pottery

Look at these Ancient Greek vases. Write captions for the first three.
In the last box, draw a Greek vase to show what the caption says

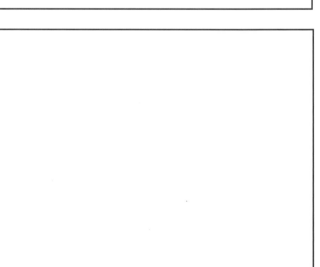

Here are people gathering olives from a tree.

PHOTOCOPIABLE

Using evidence

History objective
- To find out what sources tell us about the Olympic Games in ancient Greek times.

Resources

- Large-scale map of Ancient Greece and the surrounding islands (Generic sheet 2 – page 36)
- Pictures of statues of athletes, such as the discus thrower
- Generic sheets 5, 6, 8 (page 39, 40 and 42)
- Activity sheets 1–3 (pages 51–53)

Starting points: *whole class*

Revise briefly the sources that have been used to tell us about life in everyday Ancient Greece. Remind the children about the archaeological finds referred to in Lesson 1. Locate the venues of important sporting events like Olympia, Delphi and Corinth and mark them on the map of Greece. Display additional illustrations and diagrams of these sites, if possible.

Show the children Generic sheet 5, which illustrates athletes taking part in different events in the ancient Olympic Games. (The third picture on the right in the top row depicts a long jumper – they would jump from a standing position, the weights in the hands helping to carry them forwards.) If possible provide pictures of statues of athletes such as discus throwers for the children to see. Explain that records of the Games were written down and that the Greeks were among the first people to put together written histories. Records have been found that refer to the champions at Olympia between 776BC and AD217. Poems and stories were written about famous athletes and contests. Much of our knowledge comes from a Greek traveller called Pansanias from the second century AD. The famous Greek writer wrote the following about chariot racing at Olympia: '…at the sound of the brass trumpet off they started, all shouting to their horses and urging them on with their reins. The clatter of the rattling chariots filled the arena, and the dust flew up as they sped along in a dense mass…'

Then, using the questions and answers on Generic sheet 8, help the children begin to acquire important information about the history of the Games in Ancient Greece.

Group activities

Activity sheet 1

This activity sheet, for the least able children, involves matching pictures of some of the events featured in the ancient Olympic Games with their captions. Children will need to cut out the illustrations and the caption strips carefully and then, after matching them up, fix them on to a separate sheet of paper. Once the task is complete, encourage children to talk about the events shown in the illustrations.

Activity sheet 2

Drawings of four events from the ancient Olympic Games are featured on this activity sheet. They are chariot racing, wrestling, horse racing and hoplite running. Hoplite was the name given to infantry or foot soldiers in Greek armies. In this event soldiers were expected to run carrying a shield and to be wearing some armour like a helmet and greaves (leg guards). Space is provided under each of the illustrations for children to write their own information about what they can see. A word bank is provided to help children with appropriate vocabulary. As an extension task the children could be asked to choose another two events and to describe them through drawings and writing.

Activity sheet 3

This activity sheet, for more able children, gives them the opportunity to increase their knowledge of the events featured in the ancient Olympic Games by carrying out their own research. Sources of information should be made available to help them.

Plenary session

Reinforce children's knowledge of the events that took place in the ancient Olympic Games by holding an informal mime session. Invite children or pairs of children to come to the front of the classroom and, standing still, act out one of the events that would have been held in the Games, such as javelin throwing, long jump or boxing. Use different children until all the events have been covered.

Ideas for support

Plenty of help will be needed with spelling and vocabulary as many of the words are originally from the Greek such as *stade* (where our word stadium comes from), *hippodrome, pentathlon, pankration, hoplite, archaeologists, Zeus, discus* and *javelin*. Make a classroom display of these words so children have a constant reference.

Ideas for extension

On the school playing field, measure a *stade*, the standard unit for running races in the ancient Olympic Games (192 metres). Let the children run this distance in small groups to see how they perform. Compare their times. They could also try the *diaulos* (two lengths) and, for the ambitious, the *dolichos* (24 lengths). Ask the children to describe what it would have been like to be a winner.

Sometimes winners were rewarded with odes or poems that had been written about them. Encourage the children to write some of their own.

After researching the layout of the site at Olympia, children could make a plan drawing or construct a model to show what it looked like.

The Olympic Games was held in honour of the god Zeus. Encourage the children to find out more about him and the other chief gods of Ancient Greece.

Linked ICT activities

Talk to the children about the different types of games they play at home and the types of games they play at school. How are they different and why? Do they play more outdoor games at home? Together make a list of all the games they play at home and at school. Then write another list of the games they play outside and inside. Talk about the outdoor games they play in school and the types of games and spots they play and compete in. Think about sports day and the different sports the children take part in. Ask the children which are their favourite sports to take part in on sports day. Make a list with the children of all the different sports on sports day and ask the children to put a tick against their favourite.

Now using the computer program 'Counter for Windows', select the program within this, called 'Counter'. Type in the same information on the chart and use the bar chart facility and the pie chart to answer questions based on the information displayed. Discuss with the children how quickly this information was found out using the computer. What do they think computers may be used for at the Olympic games that take place today. How do they think the Greeks would have managed without computers to help them store the information?

Name _____

Using evidence

Look at these pictures of the Olympic Games in Ancient Greece.
Cut out the pictures and the captions and match them.

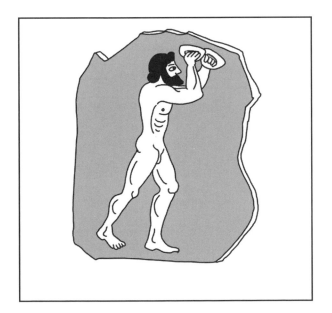

racing in armour	discus throwing
running races	long jump

Name _____

Using evidence

Here are some pictures of events in the ancient Olympic Games.
Write about each picture. Use the word bank to help you.

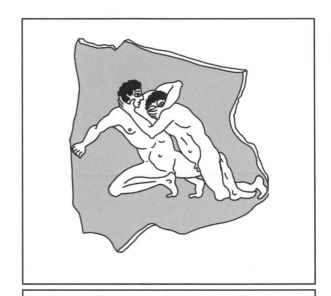

wrestling, armour, chariot, wheels, horses, shield, helmet, gallop,

greaves, steer, sprint, fight, soldier, rider

Name _____

Using evidence

Here are some pictures of events in the ancient Olympic Games.
Find out more about them and then write about each picture.

_____   _____
_____   _____
_____   _____
_____   _____

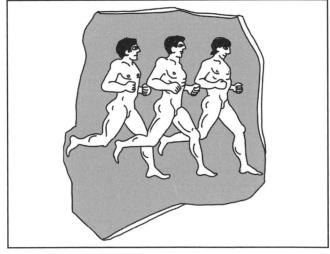

_____   _____
_____   _____
_____   _____
_____   _____

3

LESSON PLAN

Then and now

Resources

- Large-scale map of Ancient Greece and the surrounding islands (Generic sheet 2 – page 36)
- Pictures of statues of athletes, such as the discus thrower
- Scissors and glue
- Generic sheets 5, 6, 8 and 9 (page 39, 40, 42 and 43)
- Activity sheets 1–3 (pages 56–58)

Starting points: *whole class*

Display the map of Ancient Greece on which in the last lesson you marked Olympia, Delphi and Corinth (Generic sheet 2). Remind the children that these were the sites of games that were held in Ancient Greece but that the most famous was Olympia.

Use the questions and answers on Generic sheet 8 to remind the children about the ancient Games and those on Generic sheet 9 to tell them about the Games today.

Show them again the sheet that illustrates athletes taking part in different events in the ancient Olympic Games (Generic sheet 5). Remind them that pictures like these were found on pottery made by the Ancient Greeks. Show them as many other resources as you can that illustrate the ancient Games, such as statues of athletes and pictures of the remains at Olympia from reference books and CD-Roms.

Talk about the different disciplines shown in the pictures. What do the children think they are doing? Do they think they could do that sport?

Next look at the pictures on Generic sheet 6. What sports are shown here? Tell the children that they are going to look at some pictures of Ancient Greek sports and sports we do today and decide which pictures are of which Games.

Group activities

Activity sheet 1

This activity sheet, for the less able children, involves looking at pictures of some of the events featured in the ancient Olympic Games and modern Olympic Games. Using the evidence decide whether each is a sport from the ancient Games or modern Games. Once the task is complete, encourage children to talk about the events shown in the illustrations. Talk about the fact that some of the sports were done both then and now. If they ticked both modern and ancient for discus and running that is not a wrong answer!

Activity sheet 2

On this sheet the children are expected to decide what sport is being shown and in which Games it was done and then complete a caption about the picture. As an extension task children are asked to choose another two events and to describe them through drawings and writing.

Activity sheet 3

This activity sheet, for more able children, contains many more images of the sports undertaken and asks the children to devise a chart on which to display them so that they show whether they were undertaken in the ancient Games or the modern Games.

Plenary session

Draw up lists and/or displays of the events included in the ancient Olympic games and the games held now and contrast the two. Which events have stayed more or less unchanged? Which have disappeared? Which are entirely new and which entirely different? Discuss with the children which of the ancient/modern events they would like to take part in. Ask for reasons.

Ideas for support

Encourage plenty of discussion of the illustrations used, to draw out the main differences between the ancient and modern events. Point out the different styles shown in the illustrations. The Greeks used statues and decorated pots to show scenes from life and the games. Today we can use photographs, illustrations, television pictures, videos or CD-Roms.

Ideas for extension

Some children could be challenged to research the differences between other aspects of then and now, such as clothes, schooling, food, transport and so on.

Linked ICT activities

Use the internet to research information about the Olympic Games and about the different gods of Ancient Greece.

Talk to the children about creating a certificate for the winner of an event. Show them some different types of certificates and ask them to bring some in from home for a class display. Show them how to use a word processing program that allows you to import pictures. Use the pictures from the different websites to import into the word processing document. Talk about what else should be on the certificate. They may want to choose a picture of a famous athlete. Use the certificates for the school sports day.

Please note
Many of these websites by the very nature of the subject 'Greek Gods' will contain some nudity. Teachers should be aware of this when searching for these sites and that they may be blocked from use by the firewall system being used either at the school or within the LEA.

Name _____

Then and now

Look at these pictures of the Olympic Games. Put a tick in the box below each one to show whether you think it is an ancient or modern sport.

Ancient ☐
Modern ☐

Ancient ☐
Modern ☐

Ancient ☐
Modern ☐

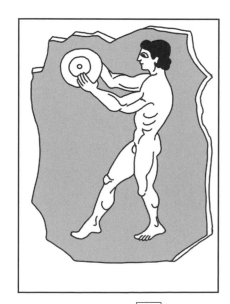

Ancient ☐
Modern ☐

Ancient ☐
Modern ☐

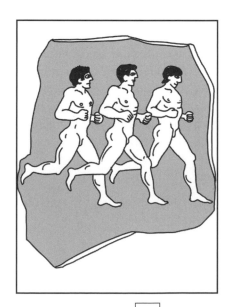

Ancient ☐
Modern ☐

Name _____

Then and now

Look at these pictures of the Olympic Games. Complete the caption saying whether you think it is an ancient or modern sport, or both.

This sport is called _____ and is ancient/modern.

This sport is called _____ and is ancient/modern.

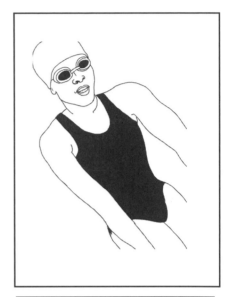

This sport is called _____ and is ancient/modern.

This sport is called _____ and is ancient/modern.

This sport is called _____ and is ancient/modern.

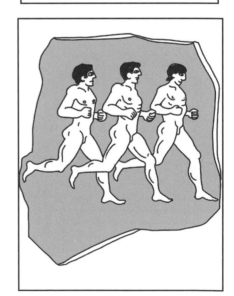

This sport is called _____ and is ancient/modern.

Name _____

Then and now

ACTIVITY SHEET 3

Look at these sports done in the Olympic Games. On another sheet make a chart to show which games are modern, which are ancient and which are both. Cut out the pictures and stick them in the right place on the chart.

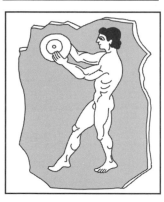

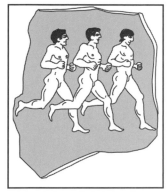

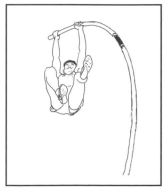

58   CURRICULUM FOCUS • FAMOUS EVENTS

PHOTOCOPIABLE

The Gunpowder Plot

CHAPTER 3

TEACHERS' NOTES

Background

Almost 400 years ago, people in Britain lived in troubled times. Religious tolerance was not like it is today. Now we are free to worship any god we choose. In those days the ruling monarch told people that they must belong to the Church of England.

The Church of England had been established during the reign of Henry VIII when the Catholic Church refused to sanction Henry's divorce from Catherine of Aragon so that he could marry Anne Boleyn. Since that time, Catholics and Protestants, as they were called, had argued passionately about their different religious beliefs. One of the most contentious issues was who should be the head of the English Church. Catholics thought it should be the Pope in Rome while Protestants believed it should be the king or queen of England. The differences in beliefs of the two churches could be summarised as in the table below.

Catholic	Protestant/C of E
Pope as head of Church	King as head of Church
Services in Latin	Services in English
Bible in Latin	Bible in English
Priest as intermediary	Direct line to God
Ornate churches	Simpler, plain churches

By the time James I succeeded Elizabeth I to become the first of the Stuart kings in 1603, Catholics had been suffering badly for some time. James I was a Protestant and for a number of reasons he had no desire to improve the conditions under which Catholics lived. He made vague promises to Catholics allowing them to worship as they wished but they were never followed through.

During the early years of his reign, Catholic church services were banned and followers were fined heavily if they did not attend Church of England services. Failure to pay these fines resulted in imprisonment. There were strict laws about Catholics training for professional positions such as doctors and lawyers and travel rights were sometimes restricted. Clandestine meetings were often held in private houses and, when they were searched, clergymen were forced to hide away in secret rooms, cupboards and passageways called 'priest holes'. Catholic priests were hunted down and sometimes killed.

The central characters

King James I

James I became King of England in 1603 because he was the nearest living relative of Elizabeth I. Described as 'the wisest fool in Christendom', he gave the impression of being a scholar but could act foolishly. James believed fervently that kings were appointed by God and could rule largely as they wished. Paintings show him to be a small, rather awkward man with rolling eyes and spindly legs. He spoke with a strong Scottish accent and is said to have had some difficulty talking clearly because his tongue seemed to be too big for his mouth. His mother was Mary, Queen of Scots and his father Lord Darnley. He became James VI of Scotland when he was only a few months old. James was extravagant and spent lavishly on his social life, particularly hunting and feasting. He was keen to avoid England being involved in expensive wars abroad and later in his reign increased his income by raising taxes on goods imported into the country. In 1611, James banished Parliament and attempted to rule the country entirely on his own. This only made the situation between monarch and Parliament worse and the methods he used to raise money were always unpopular.

Guy Fawkes

Born in the city of York in 1570, Guy Fawkes moved at the age of nine to live in a village near York when his father died and his mother married again. Guy's stepfather was Catholic and the young Fawkes made a number of Catholic friends at boarding school. Several of them went on to become priests. Guy was impressed with the way

Catholics were brave enough to stand up for what they believed, and encouraged by this he became a Catholic himself. At the age of 21 he inherited land from his father but within a year or so he had sold it to become a soldier in Holland and Belgium, where he fought for the armies of the Catholic King Philip of Spain. During the course of these campaigns, many fortified towns needed to be attacked and captured. Strong walls had to be blown up with gunpowder, so Guy Fawkes, by this time promoted to the rank of captain, soon became an expert in setting up and detonating explosives. In 1596, following his actions at the siege of Calais, he was put in charge of a company of soldiers.

Throughout his time abroad Guy kept in touch with his Catholic friends at home. Some had become poor because of the repeated fines imposed on them while others languished in prison. On one occasion, after being joined by a friend, Thomas Winter, the two Englishmen travelled across France and through Spain to Madrid to ask King Philip if he would help the plight of the Catholics in England by at least pleading their case. Philip refused to help at all and Guy and Thomas faced the long journey back completely dejected. It was not long after this that the plot to blow up James I and the noblemen began to take shape.

Robert Catesby

Instrumental in the formation of the plot was Robert Catesby, a handsome and popular young man. He owned lands and property in Warwickshire and had already been involved in other plots against the monarch. These included the Earl of Essex's unsuccessful rebellion against Elizabeth I in 1601. Elizabeth had persecuted Robert's father, Sir William Catesby, for refusing to conform to the Church of England. On another occasion, Robert Catesby was sent to the Tower of London but was saved from execution by Elizabeth. In order to pay large fines he was forced to sell some of his property. Catesby was a strong leader. He was well respected by other leading Catholics in England although his strength of character tended to dominate them. Following the death of his wife Catherine and his father there was no strong influence to hold him back.

Catesby and the fellow conspirators began to meet as early as January 1604. With Catesby as the chief instigator they began to decide on a plan of action. Among the other leading plotters, many of whom

had been school friends, were Thomas Percy, John and Christopher Wright and Thomas and Robert Winter. Guy Fawkes was engaged as the explosives expert. The men held a series of meetings in different parts of the country and as a security measure Catesby made them all swear an oath of secrecy. Catesby was always concerned about lack of money to finance the scheme and as a result the plot was widened to take in other less reliable characters.

Robert Cecil

Also playing a leading role in the story was Robert Cecil, later to become Lord Salisbury. Cecil acted as the chief minister for both Elizabeth I and James I. His father, Lord Burghley, had also been a chief minister and for some time the two of them worked together. Although frail in stature, Cecil was a clever, hard-working man who in effect ran the country. He had no time for those who disliked the monarch and other dissidents. This resulted in the harsh regulations he helped to organise against Catholics. Cecil was also the spymaster of his generation in that he ran a substantial network of spies, often referred to as 'intelligencers', to keep him informed of events both at home and abroad. It was through these spies that he found out much about the Gunpowder Plot or the 'Powder Treason' as it was known then and who was implicated in it.

Some historians in recent years have suggested that Cecil may have initiated the whole plot in order to discredit Catholics once and for all. There seems little substance in this theory. More believable is the fact that he knew about the plot while it was still in its infancy but allowed it to progress right up until the evening of 4 November when the first arrests started to be made. By this stage not only were more conspirators involved but the incident had now become a major rebellion that could be used to stir up anti-Catholic feeling throughout the country.

The main events

The plot hatched by the conspirators had essentially two parts. The first was to blow up the House of Lords on 5 November 1605 as the King and his lords met for the opening day of Parliament. Simultaneously there would be an uprising in the Midlands that would help to establish a new monarch on the throne following the death of James I. It might possibly be one of

James' two sons, Henry or Charles, or even his daughter Elizabeth (eventually she might marry a Catholic Spanish prince).

As a first step, the plotters hired premises next to the Houses of Parliament and tried to dig a tunnel under the House of Lords. It was a busy area of London, full of shops, houses and inns, and the plotters were able to move around easily without arousing suspicion. Guy Fawkes moved in as caretaker using the assumed name of John Johnson. They intended to place a large number of barrels of gunpowder under the chamber. Once these were ignited, they would cause a massive explosion killing the king and his Parliament.

The digging proved to be difficult going, especially as some of the walls and floors were up to three metres thick. They took it in turns to dig but still found it backbreaking and made slow progress. Then, by a stroke of good fortune, they discovered that a cellar next door, immediately underneath Parliament itself, had become vacant. A coal merchant had used it but he had decided to move out. The conspirators stopped digging, rented the cellar and, under cover of darkness, smuggled in over 30 barrels of gunpowder concealed under firewood and other materials. Fawkes continued to keep watch over the gunpowder while the others waited for the fateful day to arrive.

While they were waiting, the decision was taken to include others in the plot. The main reason for this appears to have been money, as the chief conspirators were finding it expensive to remain in hiding. The weak link appears to have been Francis Tresham – according to some accounts the thirteenth person to have been accepted into the circle of plotters. When Tresham realised his brothers-in-law would be attending the opening of Parliament he panicked and feared for their safety. An anonymous letter, possibly from Tresham, was sent to one of the brother-in-laws, Lord Monteagle, warning him about the dangers of attending Parliament on 5 November. The letter was soon shown to the King and Robert Cecil and a search of all the Parliament buildings, including the cellars, was organised. Monteagle was later rewarded for his loyalty and swift action with gifts of land and money.

On the night of 4 November Guy Fawkes had moved into the cellar containing the gunpowder.

He was in the dangerous process of setting the fuse needed to make the gunpowder explode the following day when voices could be heard. There was nowhere for him to escape and soon lanterns lit up the darkness. Soldiers discovered the barrels of gunpowder and almost without a struggle he was overpowered and arrested.

Taken to the Tower of London and later questioned by King James himself, Fawkes showed no remorse and refused to say he was sorry for what he had done. He admitted that if he had not been found he would have lit the gunpowder and blown up the King and Parliament. Catesby and some of the other plotters fled from London on horseback and tried to take refuge in the Midlands. For a long time after his arrest, Fawkes claimed his real name was John Johnson and he would not name his fellow conspirators. But eventually, after torture on the rack, he gave the soldiers the names they wanted. The plotters who had got away from London were tracked down to Holbeach House in Worcestershire where, after a brief skirmish, four men were shot including Catesby and Thomas Percy. The others were captured and taken back to the capital to stand trial for treason. The uprising that should have taken place in this part of the country therefore never took place.

The trial for treason was only likely to produce one verdict and Fawkes and the other conspirators were sentenced to death. They were executed by being hung, drawn and quartered in January 1606 after suffering the public humiliation of being dragged through streets packed with jeering crowds. Ironically, Fawkes was executed in Old Palace Yard, Westminster, opposite the very building he had intended to destroy. The heads of the plotters were displayed on stakes in the centre of London as a warning to anyone who would plot against the King.

Aftermath

On the night of 5 November the King's supporters celebrated his escape from treachery by making a 'guy' out of straw and burning it on a large bonfire. The King also did not want people to forget this important date. He said that at the same time each year, people should light fires and say prayers to thank God that the plot had failed. Members of Parliament passed a law that established 5 November as a day of national thanksgiving. This is why people still burn a 'guy' on a bonfire and let off fireworks into the night sky to remind them of the events that might have happened on 5 November 1605. A further extension of the tradition is the annual search made of the cellars of the Houses of Parliament by the Yeomen of the Guard before the State Opening of Parliament in November.

James I, first of the Stuart monarchs, went on to rule for another 19 relatively trouble-free years. The plot had made him even more afraid of Catholics and he continued to suppress them during the rest of his reign. James died from a stroke in 1625 at the age of 59 and was succeeded by his second son, Charles I.

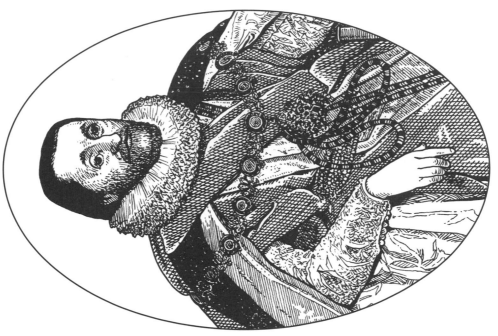

King James I

The Gunpowder Plot

The plotters

The Houses of Parliament in 1600

The Gunpowder Plot

Translation of the letter sent to Lord Monteagle ten days before the opening of Parliament was due in 1605. It was unsigned.

'My lord. Out of the love I bear to some of your friends I have a care of your preservation. Therefore I would advise you, as you tender your life, to devise some excuse to shift your attendance at this Parliament, for God and man hath concurred to punish the wickedness of this time. And think not slightly of this advertisement but retire yourself into your country, where you may expect the event in safety. For though there be no appearance of any stir, yet I say they shall receive a terrible blow this parliament, and yet they shall not see who hurts them. This counsel is not to be condemned, because it may do you good and can do you no harm, for the danger is passed as soon as you have burnt the letter and I hope God will give you the grace to make good use of it, to whose holy protection I commend you.'

A well-known rhyme used to help people remember the events of the Gunpowder Plot in 1605.

Please to remember, the fifth of November,
Gunpowder, treason and plot,
We know no reason why gunpowder treason
Should ever be forgot.

The Gunpowder Plot

Glossary of terms connected with the Gunpowder Plot story

Anonymous letter — A letter that is not signed by the person who wrote it.

Beliefs — The ideas that people think and believe to be right.

Catholic — A person who is a member of the Catholic Church. It is headed by the Pope in Rome.

Conspiracy — A plot involving a number of people to carry out some kind of plan or scheme, usually illegal.

Execution — Being put to death for carrying out a very serious crime.

Fines — Money that has to be paid as part of a punishment.

Fuse — A long lead that is lit and burns slowly. When the flame reaches the gunpowder it causes it to explode.

Gunpowder — A chemical powder that explodes easily when it is lit.

Houses of Parliament — The buildings in the Palace of Westminster, London, where laws are made and passed. There are two houses now, the House of Lords and the House of Commons.

James I — King of England from 1603 to 1625. He had already been King of Scotland since 1567.

Oath — A serious promise to keep something secret.

Pope — The leader of the Catholic Church. He lives in the Vatican in Rome.

Priest hole — A small room or cupboard where a Catholic priest could hide if anyone came.

Protestant — A member of the Church of England, who recognises the King or Queen of England as head of the Church.

Rent — The money paid to use a house or other property.

Torture — To hurt someone either to punish them or to obtain information from them.

Tower of London — A large, strong building in London once used as a prison. It is now a museum.

Treason — A crime against a country or its ruler.

The Houses of Parliament today

CURRICULUM FOCUS • FAMOUS EVENTS

Questions and answers

- **Why do we remember the fifth of November?** It is the date when the planned explosion of parliament was due to be carried out when King James I attended the annual opening event in 1605. Because of the failure of the plot, the fifth of November has been a day of public celebration ever since.

- **What is gunpowder?** Gunpowder is one of the world's oldest explosives. The Chinese used it for fireworks and it was brought to Europe by the Arabs. It is a mixture of potassium nitrate, wood charcoal and sulphur. It fires when struck with sufficient force or when heated to about 300 degrees Celsius.

- **What is treason?** Treason in these circumstances means trying to harm the king or queen of the country to which you belong. In the seventeenth century anyone found guilty of such a crime was certain to be sentenced to death and executed. It is still considered one of the most serious crimes a person can commit.

- **What is a plot?** A plan to carry out some illegal course of action. It usually involves a number of people who meet together, often in secret, to decide on what they intend to do. Sometimes an oath or solemn promise is made requiring the plotters not to tell others what has been discussed.

- **Who was James I?** He was James VI, King of Scotland who also became James I, King of England.

- **Which family did he belong to?** He belonged to the Stuart family who became rulers of England in place of the Tudors.

- **Why did he become king?** James became King of England because Elizabeth I had no children when she died and James was her nearest relative.

- **When did he become king?** He became King of England in 1603 but he had been King of Scotland since 1567.

- **How long did he reign?** James was King of England for 22 years.

- **What sort of king was he?** Many English people were delighted to have James as king after two queens and they were glad that he did not have direct rivals for the throne. James could be arrogant and lazy and was known to give money and power to his favourites. Elizabeth had left England with large debts and James made things worse by being extravagant. Some

£20,000 was spent on his coronation and he was always looking for new ways to raise money.

- **What does the word Catholic mean?** This was the name given to Christians who were followers of the Catholic Church headed by the Pope in Rome.

- **What does the word Protestant mean?** This name was given to Christians who believed the king or queen of England should be the head of the Church. Most people in England had been Catholics until 1532 when Henry VIII left the Catholic Church and established the Church of England so that he could marry his second wife Anne Boleyn.

- **What sort of things did Catholics believe?** They believed that God wanted elaborate services and beautifully decorated churches. They wanted the Bible to remain in an ancient language called Latin.

- **What sort of things did Protestants believe?** They believed God wanted plain churches and simple forms of worship. They wanted the Bible to be written in English so that people could read it for themselves.

- **How were Catholics treated?** Catholics were ordered to attend Protestant churches. If they failed to attend they were fined large amounts of money. Catholic churches were often destroyed. Catholic priests were hunted down and sometimes killed. Some Catholics tried to hold secret services in their own houses. Special hiding places were made for priests called priest holes. If they were caught they were severely punished.

- **Who were the plotters?** The leader was Robert Catesby. Other leading plotters were Thomas Percy and two sets of brothers, John and Christopher Wright and Thomas and Robert Winter. Catesby asked Guy Fawkes to come back to England from fighting abroad, not only because he was a Catholic but also because he was an expert at using gunpowder. Later the plotters were joined by Ambrose Rookwood, Everard Digby and Francis Tresham.

- **What happened next?** The plotters met in a number of different locations over a period of months. They at first attempted to tunnel under the Houses of Parliament from a property close by but then managed to rent a cellar immediately underneath where the king would be. They smuggled more than 30 barrels of gunpowder into the cellar in readiness.

Questions and answers

- **Who wrote the letter that was sent to Lord Monteagle?** We will probably never know. The letter was unsigned. The most likely writer is Francis Tresham who seems to have joined the plotters later when extra financial help was needed. It has also been suggested that the letter may have been 'manufactured' by Robert Cecil himself in order to force the king to take action.

- **When was the letter sent?** Ten days before the State Opening of Parliament was due to take place.

- **Who was Lord Monteagle?** One of Tresham's brothers-in-law, William Parker, Lord Monteagle, who was due to be present on the occasion when the king went to open parliament.

- **What did the letter say?** (A simplified version is on Generic sheet 2.) It did not spell out the plot in detail but it was not difficult to infer what it meant. It spoke of 'having a care for the preservation' of Monteagle, and urging him to find an excuse not to attend and to 'retire into your country'. Parliament, it said, would 'receive a terrible blow' but would 'not see who hurts them'.

- **What happened to the letter?** Monteagle decided the king should be informed. He rode to London immediately and showed it to James' chief minister Robert Cecil. Monteagle was later rewarded with money and land for doing this.

- **What was the outcome?** James realised that someone was planning to kill him. He ordered a search of the buildings surrounding the Houses of Parliament. The search of the cellar under the Houses of Parliament was carried out late on the evening of 4 November 1605 when Fawkes and the gunpowder were found.

- **How would Fawkes have felt when he heard the soldiers coming?** Although a brave soldier who had fought in a number of battles, Fawkes must have felt frightened when the soldiers appeared as he knew there was no real explanation for the gunpowder and that once questioned he would not be able to escape.

- **What happened next?** Once the gunpowder had been discovered, Fawkes was arrested without much of a struggle. A fuse was also discovered leading to the barrels of gunpowder. Once lit, it would have given Fawkes about 15 minutes to get clear of the building.

- **Where was Fawkes taken?** To the king's bedchamber for preliminary questioning. He did not apologise for what he had intended to do. He said that had he not been discovered he would have gone ahead with the plan later that day. Once questioning had been completed, he was taken to the Tower of London.

- **What happened to him there?** When Fawkes would not name the other plotters, which gave some of them time to get away, torture was used. This was common practice in those days. Among the tortures used was the rack, which stretched the body. Eventually he named the others and was forced to sign a confession. Fawkes' signature on various documents got more shaky as the torture continued.

- **What happened in the Midlands?** With Fawkes not naming the other plotters at the start, a number of them escaped to the Midlands where a rebellion was due to break out. They sheltered at Holbeach Hall in Worcestershire where they were found by the king's men. Some, including Catesby and Thomas Percy, were killed in the attack. Others were captured and taken to the Tower of London.

- **What happened to Fawkes and the rest of the plotters?** They were put on trial in London towards the end of January 1606. Their confessions were read out. All eight were sentenced to death for high treason and returned to the Tower of London, going in through Traitor's Gate. Everard Digby, Robert Winter, John Grant and Thomas Bates were executed on 29 January 1606 in St Paul's Churchyard. The next day the same fate followed for Thomas Winter, Robert Keyes, Guy Fawkes and Ambrose Rookwood but this time in the Old Palace Yard, Westminster. Their heads were displayed in public to warn others. Further trials and executions followed later. Francis Tresham, the possible writer of the anonymous letter, was kept in the Tower and died there of natural causes.

PHOTOCOPIABLE

Questions and answers

- **What did King James say after the attempt to kill him?** He said that at the same time each year, 5 November, people should celebrate by lighting fires. They should also say prayers of thanks that the plot had failed to kill him.

- **What did the Members of Parliament do?** The Members of Parliament passed a law stating that 5 November should be a day of national thanksgiving and that the celebrations should be held on the same day every year afterwards.

- **Why do we make model 'guys'?** The name 'guy' comes from Guy Fawkes, the conspirator who, even though he was not the leader, was given the job of remaining in the cellar under the Houses of Parliament and lighting the fuse to produce the gunpowder explosion. Before his execution Fawkes and the other main plotters were paraded through the streets of London so people got to know what they looked like. People made effigies of Guy Fawkes to burn on the bonfires when celebrations were held later.

- **What is the purpose of the fireworks?** The main purpose of the fireworks appears to be to recreate the kind of explosions that would have been set off when the barrels of gunpowder exploded.

- **What is the purpose of the bonfire?** The exploding gunpowder would have caused the Houses of Parliament to catch fire and burn. Burning the 'guy' on a bonfire is also intended to be a symbolic way of destroying the plot that was made against the king.

- **What happens at the State Opening of Parliament?** Members of both Houses of Parliament, the Lords and the Commons, gather together and the Queen, dressed appropriately in jewels and crown, reads through a prepared statement of the programme of laws the government of the day intends to carry out in the year to come. Before the State Opening it is a tradition that a search of the Houses of Parliament is still carried out.

- **Who carries out this search?** Today the search is carried out by the Yeomen of the Guard in their traditional uniforms of red and black, which are a survival from Tudor times. The Yeomen of the Guard are an ancient royal bodyguard recruited from old soldiers. Those at the Tower of London are distinct from the guard proper and have permanent duties. The Yeomen of the Guard are sometimes referred to as 'beefeaters'. The word comes from the French buffetier – the man who served at the royal buffet or table.

The Gunpowder Plot

History objectives
- To understand what the Gunpowder Plot was.
- To find out about the people who were involved in it.

Resources

- Class timeline
- A large black hat and a golden crown
- Rulers and coloured pencils
- Generic sheets 1–5 (pages 63–67)
- Activity sheets 1–3 (pages 72–74)

Starting points: *whole class*

Introduce the story of the Gunpowder Plot by asking the children what they know about Bonfire Night. Teach them the rhyme about the fifth of November (see Generic sheet 2). Ask if anyone knows it already if they can explain what it means. Put the rhyme up on the flipchart or whiteboard and run through it several times until the children can recite it without help. Talk about some of the words and phrases in the rhyme (see also the glossary on Generic sheet 3). Refer to the teachers' notes and the questions and answers on Generic sheet 5.

Explain that we remember the fifth of November because that was when the planned explosion of parliament using gunpowder was due to be carried out when King James I attended the annual opening event in 1605. Because of the failure of the plot, the fifth of November has been a day of public celebration ever since.

Tell the children the start of the story surrounding the Gunpowder Plot – that the plotters wanted to kill the king because they felt he was unkind to them and wouldn't let them practise their religion in the way they wanted to. Display the picture of the plotters (Generic sheet 1). Explain that this event happened towards the end of 1605. Locate the event on the large class timeline (Chapter 2, Generic sheet 3). Show how it relates in sequence to the other events covered in this book (well after the birth of the Olympic Games but a bit before the Great Fire of London).
Display the picture of James I from Generic sheet 1

and discuss with the children key questions about him. (See the questions and answers on Generic sheet 5.)

Tell the children they will now do an activity in which they have to use pictures to put the story in the order that it happened.

Group activities

Activity sheet 1
These children have four pictures to match with captions, cut out and put in the order that the story happened.

Activity sheet 2
These children have six pictures to match with captions, cut out and put in the order that the story happened. The captions have missing words that the children must write in.

Activity sheet 3
These children have six pictures to write captions for, then cut out and put in the order that the story happened. Provide them with paper for writing the captions.

Plenary session

Ask two prepared adults to help you, one playing one of the plotters such as Guy Fawkes and the other King James. Guy Fawkes should wear the large black hat and James I the golden crown. Put them 'in the hot seat' and let the children ask them questions about the story so far. For example, questions to ask Guy Fawkes: What was it like being a soldier? Why did you want to blow up the king? How easy was it to get the gunpowder into the cellar? Questions to ask the king: What was it like to be king? Why didn't you like Catholics? Why were you going to the Houses of Parliament?

Ideas for support

Plenty of discussion will be needed about the contrasting views held by Protestants and Catholics throughout the Gunpowder Plot story. A chart of the main differences is provided in the background notes on page 59. This could be copied and displayed in the classroom. Also work on key vocabulary and terms that need to be understood in order to fully appreciate the course of events.

Ideas for extension

Find out about other aspects of the reign of James I and what life was like for ordinary people in Britain at that time. What sort of houses did they live in? How did they dress? What sort of work did they do? How did they entertain themselves? Also look at other historical events of the time like the dispute between James and the Puritans and the voyage of the Pilgrim Fathers to settle in America in 1620.

Linked ICT activities

Talk to the children about the ways in which they might celebrate different events, including bonfire night, during the year. Talk about celebrating a religious occasion, such as Christmas or Divali, their own birthday and any special days they may have in school (sports day, school open day). Talk about how we let people know that these events are taking place. Discuss the idea of sending invitations out to invite people to come to an event. Show them different types of invitations, such as for a wedding or a party, and encourage them to bring in any they may have at home for a class display.

Using any word processing program that allows you to create a word bank, such as 'Talking Write Away', 'Textease' and 'Clicker 4', create a word bank with words that will help the children to write an invitation to parents and friends to a bonfire party at the school on bonfire night. Encourage them to use the internet to look for different pictures that they may want to include as part of the invitation. Talk about the different information that would be needed as part of the invitation – where the event will take place, what time and how much it would cost to attend.

Name _____

The plot

Cut out the pictures and captions. Match the pictures to captions and then put them in the order the story happened.

King James said people could not be Catholics.

The plotters planned to kill the king.

Guy Fawkes put gunpowder in the Houses of Parliament.

The king's men found Guy Fawkes and arrested him.

The plot

Fill in the missing words in the captions then cut out the captions and the pictures and put them in the order the story happened.

Guy Fawkes was a _____.

The _____ could not escape.

King _____ said people could not be Catholics.

The plotters planned to _____ the king.

Guy _____ put gunpowder in the _____ of Parliament.

The king's men found _____ Fawkes and arrested him.

Name _____

The plot

Below are pictures of the story of the Gunpowder Plot. On another sheet of paper, write a caption for each picture using the words in the box to help you. Then cut out the pictures and captions and place them in the order the story happened.

Fawkes • plotters • Houses of Parliament • soldier
gunpowder • arrested • treason

Then and now

History objectives
• To understand the difference between then and now.

Resources

- Generic sheets 1, 2, 4 and 6 (pages 63, 64, 66 and 68)
- Activity sheets 1–3 (pages 77–79)
- Sticky notes

Starting points: *whole class*

Show the children the picture of the present-day Houses of Parliament on Generic sheet 4. Explain that it was made up of many more small buildings in 1605. Demonstrate this using the picture on Generic sheet 1. Talk about the main differences between 'then' and 'now'.

Tell the children that in 1605 there was only one part to Parliament. This was made up of noblemen or lords – rich, important people – who were not elected. Contrast this by explaining that Parliament today is made up of two parts or houses. There is still one for the lords but there is also one called the House of Commons for Members of Parliament. There are about 600 of these MPs and they are elected to go there to represent people in all the different parts of the country. Say that there is an election for MPs about every four to five years.

Also tell the children that the Queen, Elizabeth II, is still head of the British Parliament but that she only goes there once a year to open it and is not directly involved in what it does. The person in charge effectively is the Prime Minister who runs the country with the help of other important people called Ministers. Explain that events from the Houses of Parliament are shown on television most days and Ministers are often interviewed during news programmes.

If the school has a school council, make comparisons between how its members are elected and the process of electing MPs. Talk about the meaning of key words such as election, voting, secret ballot and ballot box.

Group activities

Activity sheet 1

These children have to compare the Houses of Parliament as they were then and as they are today. A word bank is provided to help them with the labelling. They should write their labels on sticky notes and stick them on the pictures. Alternatively you could cut out the pictures and stick them on to a larger sheet of paper. The labels could then be written around the pictures.

Activity sheet 2

On this activity sheet the children are provided with the same two pictures but they are required this time to write their own labels for them. They could also use a colour coding system to show the main differences between the two sets of buildings. As for Activity sheet 1, the children could use sticky notes.

Activity sheet 3

This activity sheet is for more able children. It requires them to write more detailed sentences to explain the essential differences between the buildings. These sentences may need to be written on a separate piece of paper.

Plenary session

Return to the 'in the hot seat' activity suggested for Lesson 1. Brief two adults to help. Again, one should represent James I and the other Guy Fawkes. Ask the king questions like these: How did you feel when you discovered the plot? Why did you use torture? How did you feel about Catholics afterwards? Ask Guy Fawkes questions like these: How did you feel down in the cellar? What was it like in the Tower of London? Do you think you should have been executed?

Ideas for support

Provide as much help as possible with the vocabulary needed to compare the two sets of buildings. It may be helpful to brainstorm the children's suggestions and then display the results in the classroom using the whiteboard or a flipchart. They will then be able to refer to this when they are working on the activity sheets.

Ideas for extension

Investigate the work of the Houses of Parliament today. Look at the House of Lords and the House of Commons. How are Members of Parliament elected? What work do they do? The children may be able to make contact with their own Member of Parliament.

Do the children know the name of the current Prime Minister and where he lives in London? Some research on famous Prime Ministers in the past could be carried out, for example, Second World War leader Winston Churchill and Margaret Thatcher, Britain's first female Prime Minister.

Linked ICT activities

Talk to the children about what it means to be elected as an MP and how people are put forward for elections. Show them some of the election publicity leaflets that are pushed through your door at election time. Talk about what people might write about themselves if they want to become elected. Say that they are going to have their own class election and that they are all going to create their own election publicity paper.

Start by showing the children how to use the digital camera. Let them takes turns to take a photograph of each other. Then help them to import the picture into a word processing program, such as 'Talking Write Away' or 'Textease'. Encourage them to write at least five sentences about themselves, their hobbies, what they like to do at home and their favourite subject at school. Print out the final election papers and display them in the classroom.

Encourage all the children to read about each other and at the end of the following week carry out a vote using voting papers to find out who is going to be the class MP for the week. (You could decide on some special duties that this child could then carry out as the class MP for the week.) Involve all the

children through the whole process of voting and counting the votes.

Name _____

Then and now

Look at these two pictures. Use the words in the box to write labels for both of them and stick the labels on.

The Houses of Parliament in Guy Fawkes' time.

The Houses of Parliament today.

| bridge | River Thames | tower | clock | flag | stone | roof |
| windows | Big Ben | Westminster | water | spire |

PHOTOCOPIABLE

Name _____

Then and now

Look at these two pictures. Write some labels for both of them and stick them on. Show with arrows where the main differences are.

The Houses of Parliament in Guy Fawkes' time.

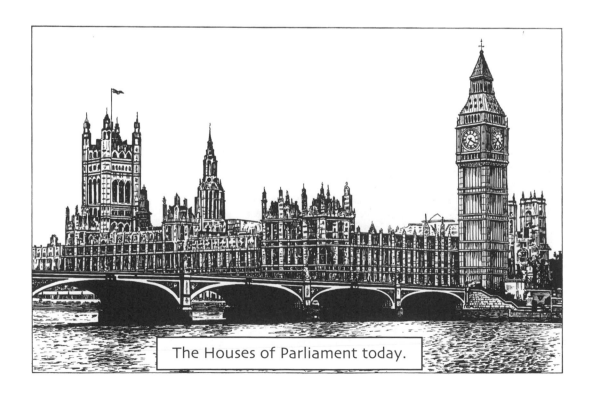

The Houses of Parliament today.

Name _____

Then and now

Look at the two pictures below. On another sheet of paper, write some sentences to explain the differences between the buildings then and today.

The Houses of Parliament in Guy Fawkes' time.

The Houses of Parliament today.

Celebrating the plot

3
LESSON PLAN

Resources

• Video extracts of the State Opening of Parliament and video player (optional)
• Flipchart or whiteboard
• Generic sheet 7 (page 69)
• Activity sheets 1–3 (pages 82–84)
• Scissors, glue and extra supplies of paper

Starting points: *whole class*

Stress to the children that following the events of the Gunpowder Plot in 1605, James I did not want people in Britain to forget what had happened. So he said that at the same time each year, 5 November, they should celebrate by lighting fires.

Explain that there are other links with the past. The State Opening of Parliament by the Queen takes place every year in early November. They could try to find out when the event is due to happen next and try to watch extracts of it on television. Parts of the ceremony could be viewed 'live' or it could be recorded on video and selected extracts watched later.

Talk about how the Queen reads through a prepared statement of the programme of laws that the government of the day intends to carry out in the year to come. Say that before this event it is a tradition that a search of the Houses of Parliament is still carried out.

Use the questions and answers on Generic sheet 7 to support these discussions.

Discuss with the children the different ways in which we celebrate 5 November, Bonfire Night, these days. Talk about the 'guy', the fire and the fireworks. Do they go to an organised party? Which part of the party do they like best?

Say that today they are going to carry out activities that will look, in pictures and in words, at how we celebrate the Gunpowder Plot now.

Group activities

Activity sheet 1
This sheet is intended for children who need support with their writing. A word bank is provided to help with the labelling of the picture. There is also a simple question to answer. They should write their labels on sticky notes and stick them on the picture. Alternatively they could cut out the picture and stick it on to a larger sheet of paper. The labels could then be written around the picture.

Activity sheet 2
On this activity sheet the children are not only asked to label the picture but they also have to match the beginning of each sentence with its correct ending. Scissors, glue and extra supplies of paper will be needed to carry out the cutting and pasting task. As for Activity sheet 1, the children could use sticky notes.

Activity sheet 3
This task is aimed at more able children. After labelling the picture, children are required to complete the cloze procedure activity where they choose words from the box to fit into the correct place in the text. As for Activity sheet 1, the children could use sticky notes.

Plenary session

Check the responses children have produced and receive feedback from each of the groups using the different activity sheets. Stress the importance of safety codes when firework displays are taking place. Discuss the fact that the events being celebrated happened 400 years ago. Why is it important that we still celebrate them today? Will the date 5 November ever disappear from the calendar in the future?

Ideas for support

Talk through the activity sheets before the children start on them. Some children may benefit from more extensive word banks to help them with their labelling and writing. Reinforce the experience with colourful visual class displays showing bonfires and fireworks.

Ideas for extension

Extend the celebrations of the Bonfire Night theme in more cross-curricular ways. Experiment with short alliterative poems based on Bonfire Night where most of the words in phrases or sentences begin with the same letter; for example, 'fancy, flashing fireworks fizz'. Use paints, pastels, crayons etc to create colourful Bonfire Night pictures and posters. Reproduce firework movements in dance and drama sessions.

Linked ICT activities

Talk to the children about what they normally do on bonfire night to celebrate this day. Have a class discussion about the different types of fireworks they might see when they go to a display and the types of sounds they might hear from the fireworks.

Tell the children that they are going to create their own picture of a firework display including with the picture words which show some of the sounds that they might hear like, bang and crash, zoom and flash. Using a graphics program such as 'Dazzle', 'Fresco', Granada's 'Colours' or anything similar, show the children how to change the colour of the screen to black by filling the whole of the painting area. Then show them how to use the different drawing tools to give the different effects – the spray tool, the line tool and any other special effects tools the program may contain. Show them how to change the different colours in the program. Encourage them to experiment with the colours and the tools to create special effects on the black background so it looks like fireworks lighting up the night sky.

Finally, show the children how to use the text tool to add the different words to the bonfire scene.

Create your own firework display using the firework pictures around a large picture of Guy Fawkes.

Name _____

Bonfire night

Write some labels and stick them on the picture below.

WORD BANK

bonfire   fireworks   guy

When is bonfire night? _____

Name _____

Bonfire night

Write some labels and stick them on the picture below.

Match each sentence beginning to the correct ending.

Bonfire night is held on	set on fire.
A guy is put on top	also lit.
The bonfire is	November 5th.
Fireworks are	of the bonfire.

Name _____

Bonfire night

Write some labels and stick them on the picture below.

Choose the correct words from the box to complete these sentences.

Bonfire night is celebrated every year

on _____

A lifesize model of a man is put on top of

the _____

It is called a _____, and is

named after Guy Fawkes.

The bonfire is set on _____

and _____ are lit.

_____

bonfire
November 5th
scarecrow
rubbish
fire
fireworks
December 25th
candles
guy

PHOTOCOPIABLE

The Coronation of Queen Elizabeth II

CHAPTER 4

T E A C H E R S '   N O T E S

Background

Queen Elizabeth II (full name Elizabeth Alexandra Mary) succeeded her father, King George VI, when he died aged 56 from a heart attack early on the morning of 5 February 1952. She was the great-great-granddaughter of Queen Victoria and at 25 was the same age at which Elizabeth I had come to the throne.

There had been concerns about the health of King George VI since the summer of 1951 but there appeared to be no real problems when Princess Elizabeth and her husband, Prince Philip, left for a royal visit to Australia and New Zealand in January 1952. They stopped in Kenya to take a short safari break on the way and it was there that Elizabeth was informed of her father's death.

The couple returned to England immediately and there began three months of full mourning. By the summer of 1952 the Queen had moved into Buckingham Palace and was resuming royal duties. She attended her first State Opening of Parliament in November of that year and by then plans were already being made for the official coronation ceremony to take place some time during the early summer of 1953.

The date was finally fixed for Tuesday 2 June, some 16 months after Elizabeth had become Queen, and the location of the ceremony was to be Westminster Abbey. The date was chosen because the Meteorological Office considered it the day on which it was most unlikely to rain. They were very wrong: 2 June turned out to be a very wet day in London with a number of heavy showers and temperatures well below the seasonal average.

The delay between the accession to the throne and the coronation was blamed on the lengthy and detailed planning that needed to be carried out. The Duke of Norfolk, the Earl Marshal of England, was chosen to organise the event. A special committee was set up under the chairmanship of Prince Philip to assist him, and the Queen herself was also closely involved in the planning. It is said that when organisational problems arose the Queen would always ask 'Did my father do it?' If the reply was 'Yes' she would say 'Then I will do it.'

The coronation ceremony used in 1953 was a curious mixture of religious and pagan ritual. Back in early history, monarchs, rulers or chiefs had usually been acclaimed in a public ceremony in which they were raised on a shield, presented with a spear or sword, or invested with some distinct robe or head-dress. When Europe became Christian, aspects of these pagan symbols had been grafted on to religious services that resembled some biblical accounts of coronations like the one involving Solomon described in the Old Testament. The ceremony also contained features that had been handed down from the coronation of the Anglo-Saxon king, Edgar, at Bath in 973.

Tension rose as the big day got nearer and the organisers concentrated on the many important jobs they had to do. The Queen apparently remained unconcerned. When asked by a lady-in-waiting if she was beginning to feel nervous, she is supposed to have replied, 'Of course I am, but I really do think Aureole will win,' referring to a horse she owned that was running in the world famous race, the Derby, being run at about the same time.

Preparations

At least a week before the coronation ceremony was due to take place, London began to prepare itself for the event. By 23 May street decorations were in place. There were flags, golden arches, crowns, banners, bunting and pennants, shields and crests, lions and unicorns as London put on its coronation dress of predominantly red, white and blue. New paint was everywhere as buildings were spruced up especially for the occasion. Statues and fountains were boarded up and stands and barriers erected. People from all parts of the world began to arrive in the capital for the event. In the four days leading up to the coronation, traffic was almost at a standstill in the region immediately around Westminster Abbey and there was very little non-coronation news published in any of the newspapers.

Two days before the event, crowds of people began to bed down on the procession route in order to guarantee a good position. By dusk on Monday 1 June it was estimated that nearly half a million people were already lining the streets that the procession would follow, despite the pouring rain and the driving wind. For the lucky ones who worked for companies and businesses with premises on the route there was some shelter as offices, shops and showrooms were turned into temporary grandstands. With perfect timing, and as if to give the crowd encouragement, the news was announced that the world's highest mountain, Mount Everest, had been successfully climbed for the first time by the New Zealander Edmund Hillary and Tenzing Norgay of Nepal.

The day itself

Even spectators with official tickets for the special viewing platforms that were erected along the way had to be up very early on the day, with some being required to be in their places by six o'clock on the morning of 2 June.

British Rail laid on 6,500 special trains to London on Coronation Day and it was estimated that over 6,000 coaches also brought visitors into the capital from other parts of the UK. The statistics are interesting: 7,000 policemen were on duty, London Transport ran over 40,000 buses into central London before 8.30am on 2 June, over 8,000 first-aid workers were standing by in case of illness and accident, and over 30,000 catering staff were drafted in to run refreshment tents. It was estimated some two million people eventually lined the procession route, some standing on their chosen piece of pavement for up to 30 hours.

The final format actually chosen for Queen Elizabeth's coronation ceremony, presided over by the Archbishop of Canterbury, the Most Reverend Geoffrey Fisher, had seven main features.

1. The new queen was presented to the people for recognition – one of the oldest traditions of a coronation event.
2. She swore an oath to maintain the church, restrain crime and ensure justice.
3. The Queen was then anointed with holy oil to give her spiritual power. This was carried out in private behind a specially raised canopy.
4. Then came the actual crowning and the presentation of regalia. The crown used in the ceremony was St Edward's Crown, complete with over 400 precious and semiprecious jewels. Other regalia was also presented to the monarch at this point, including the orb (symbolising commitment to Christianity), the sword (as a mark of respect and honour) and the sceptre (representing royal authority and power). Presentations were also made of special robes, rings, bracelets and spurs.
5. This was followed by the paying of homage by the leading peers of the country.
6. Then came the invocation (the saying of special prayers).
7. Finally, once the ceremony was complete, came the banquet for important guests and other events to celebrate the occasion.

Over 13,000 troops took part in the coronation procession that followed the ceremony in Westminster Abbey. There were 27 carriages and 29 marching bands to maintain the crowds' attention along a seven-mile (11km) route that included Whitehall, Haymarket, Oxford Street, Piccadilly and The Mall (see Generic sheet 1). For those marching, the journey was to take around one and three-quarter hours. Queen Elizabeth rode in the gold state coach, dating from 1762. The 24-foot coach had been regilded for the occasion and contained panels painted by the Italian artist Giovanni Battista Cipriani. Eight horses drew the coach harnessed in red Moroccan leather.

For the procession, the Queen had replaced St Edward's Crown with the Imperial State Crown, which was lighter and considered to be more comfortable to wear. The Queen wore white satin robes designed by Norman Hartnell. The theme of the design was floral emblems and included the rose of England, the shamrock of Ireland, the thistle of Scotland and the leek of Wales. In order to appreciate fully the spectacle before them, many of the crowd used cardboard periscopes to see over the heads of those in front. These were provided free in newspapers and magazines but became obsolete when the heavy rain turned the cardboard to pulp. Once the Queen had arrived back at Buckingham Palace she made several appearances on the balcony to wave to the huge crowds who had poured down The Mall and flooded up to the gates and railings of the palace. There was a flypast of aircraft and as darkness approached, at about

9.30pm, the Queen appeared on the balcony again to switch on the 'lights of London'. A chain of bonfires was also lit from Cornwall to the north of Scotland to mark the occasion.

But it was not only in London that the coronation festivities were in full swing. It was as much a day of celebration for ordinary people as it was for the rich and famous. Coronation Day was a public holiday for most people and schools and public buildings were closed. It was the ideal opportunity for everyone to raise their spirits as post-war recovery really began to sink in. Streets and houses were decorated in villages, towns and cities throughout Britain, and many events, some which had taken over a year to be organised, were staged. There were tea parties and ox-roasts, plays and historical pageants, fancy dress and craft competitions, dances and sports, and coronation queens complete with attendants. In the evening the parties continued while many returned home to watch the whole event again on television. Over two million souvenir mugs were made and presented to schoolchildren during the day.

Prime Minister Winston Churchill, then 79 years old, summed up the day's events when he told radio listeners during the evening:

We have had a day which the oldest are proud to have lived to see and which the youngest will remember all their lives. The splendours of this second of June glow in our minds. Now as night falls you will hear the voice of our Sovereign herself crowned in our history and enthroned for ever in our hearts.

The impact of television

In 1937 the coronation procession of the Queen's father, George VI, had become the first outside broadcast to be televised by the BBC, although the transmission was restricted to the immediate area around London. Sixteen years later the viewing audience was to stretch countrywide as almost the whole of the Coronation Day ceremonies went out on screens live, despite the initial objections of the organisers. It meant the new queen would be crowned literally 'in the sight of the people'.

It was in many ways the beginning of the television age. Thousands of people bought or hired television sets to watch the event. Others crowded into the homes of friends and neighbours while many looked on from outside electrical appliance shops.

There were also big screen relays to cinemas and other public places. The number of licence holders doubled to three million and many who rented sets decided to retain them afterwards. The special coronation edition of the *Radio Times* sold over nine million copies. An estimated 27 million viewers in Britain – over half the population – watched the television broadcast for at least part of the day while live links were made to Europe, especially France, Germany and Holland. A recorded version of the event was soon on its way to countries further afield like the United States.

The average price of a television set in 1953 was around £90 – similar to the cost of a new family car – although cheaper kit forms were available for construction at home. Sets resembled items of wooden furniture like a sideboard or a chest of drawers with a screen in the middle about the size of a dinner plate to show the black and white picture.

Television commentary on the day was provided by Richard Dimbleby, a well-known radio broadcaster during the Second World War, who explained in detail the meaning of every feature of the coronation ceremony, some of which dated back thousands of years.

Postscript

The Silver Jubilee (25 years) of Queen Elizabeth's accession to the throne was celebrated in the summer of 1977. The Queen travelled to Commonwealth countries such as Australia and New Zealand, Canada and the West Indies while in Britain she covered more than 11,000km. There was a service of thanksgiving at St Paul's Cathedral in June and Prince Charles left the Royal Navy to take charge of the Queen's Silver Jubilee Trust. People sent 100,000 cards to the Queen, while Virginia Wade became a focus of the celebrations by winning the Wimbledon Lawn Tennis Ladies Singles title. Street parties, fetes and other events were held throughout the country.

For her Golden Jubilee (50 years) the Queen embarked on a tour of the regions of Britain during a period lasting several months and there were also church services to mark the occasion. Two special bank holidays were granted during the first week in June. Among the most memorable events staged at this time were two huge open-air concerts attended by the Queen and held in the grounds of

Buckingham Palace. One of the concerts was devoted to classical music while the other featured popular music from the five decades of the Queen's reign.

The fiftieth anniversary of the coronation was celebrated on 2 June 2003. A thanksgiving service in Westminster Abbey was followed by a children's party in the grounds of Buckingham Palace, complete with clowns and a bouncy castle.

The route of the coronation

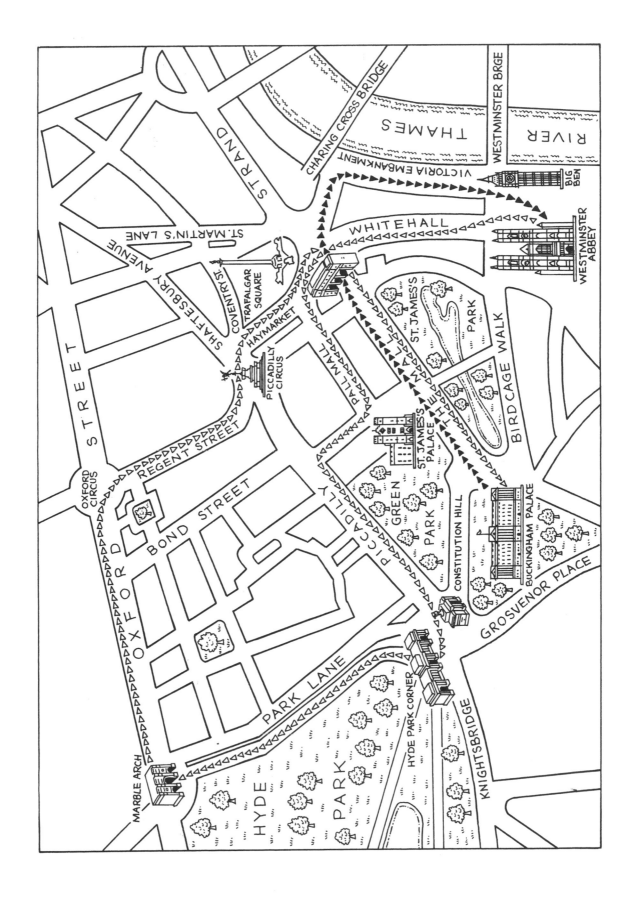

Eyewitness accounts

Watching on television

"Very few people had televisions. There was only one on the street where I lived. All the neighbours crowded into the living room of the people who owned the television to watch at different times during the day. The television set was like a piece of wooden furniture. It had a very small screen, I think it was nine inches, and the picture was a rather blurred black and white. It was the first time I had ever seen television and it was quite a long time afterwards that we first had our own."

Making money

"For three days I worked double shifts in the hotel starting at about seven in the morning and finishing at about ten o'clock at night. Although some amounts were small, over the three days as a whole I made almost £100 in tips – a fortune. When it was all over I slept for three solid days."

Day off school

"All the schoolchildren from our area had to be ready at the station by 6.45am to catch a special train into London. When the train arrived we were marched along in lines to our spot to watch the procession pass by. We were there by 7.30am and had ages to wait but the time passed quickly as there was always something happening to see and talk about."

Getting a good view

"It seemed as if all London had turned out to watch. As I was only six years old and fairly short I could see nothing because of the people in front of me. I started to cry rather loudly. A kindly soldier took pity on me and after asking my mother's permission lifted me on to his shoulders for the duration of the procession."

Street parties

"My brother and I got up very early. People had been looking forward to the day and preparing street parties. All the streets were decorated with flags and bunting and pictures of the royal family. First we watched the service on television and then went back to enjoy a noisy street party. All the neighbours provided the food and drink."

Fancy dress competitions

"The children's costumes all had to be home-made for the competition. They all lined up in the parade. There were princes, princesses, knights in armour, kings, queens and fairies. Suddenly it started to rain hard. All the paper went soggy and the paint began to run. Everyone ended up in a dreadful state."

In the 1950s

Elizabeth II

A timeline of the main events in her life

1926 Princess Elizabeth born in London.

1936 Elizabeth's father becomes king when his older brother decides to step down.

1930s She is taught at home by tutors rather than at school. She becomes a Girl Guide when she is 11.

1940 She sends a radio message to the children of Britain during the Second World War.

1942 First public engagement. She inspects soldiers of the Grenadier Guards on her 16th birthday.

1947 First official overseas visit. Celebrates 21st birthday in South Africa.

1947 On 20 November she marries Prince Philip at Westminster Abbey. He is the son of Prince Andrew of Greece.

1948 Her first child, Prince Charles, is born.

1950 Her second child, Princess Anne, is born.

1952 Her father, King George VI, dies and she becomes Queen.

1953 On 2 June her coronation takes place in Westminster Abbey.

1960 Prince Andrew is born.

1964 Prince Edward is born.

1977 The Queen's Silver Jubilee is celebrated (25 years).

1982 Prince William, son of Prince Charles and the next heir to the throne after Charles, is born. The Queen is now 56 years old.

1992 A bad fire wrecks part of one of the Queen's homes, Windsor Castle.

1997 Princess Diana is killed in Paris in a car crash.

2002 The Queen's Golden Jubilee is celebrated (50 years).

2003 Celebration of the fiftieth anniversary of her coronation.

PHOTOCOPIABLE

Questions and answers

- **What is a coronation?**

  It is a special ceremony when a king or queen is crowned as ruler or monarch of their country. It is an ancient ceremony. The coronation of Queen Elizabeth II was based on ceremonies performed for previous kings and queens of England but also on coronations described in the Old Testament of the Bible.

- **When did Queen Elizabeth's coronation take place?**

  The event took place on 2 June 1953 – 16 months after Elizabeth had become Queen when her father died on 5 February 1952. The Golden Jubilee celebrations held in 2002 were 50 years from the date of the accession to the throne not the coronation.

- **Who organised it?**

  Chief organiser of the coronation event was a high-ranking nobleman called the Duke of Norfolk. He held the title of Earl Marshal of England. There was also a special coronation committee that was set up to help him. The chairman of this committee was Prince Philip, the Queen's husband.

- **Where did it happen?**

  The main celebrations were held in London. The Queen's procession started and finished at her home, Buckingham Palace. The coronation ceremony was held in Westminster Abbey.

- **Who was there?**

  Only people who had special invitations could go. All the Queen's family were there, lords and ladies and important people from the country, including Members of Parliament. There were many kings, queens, prime ministers and rulers from other countries. A number of seats were also made available for ordinary people from Britain so that they too could see the Queen crowned.

- **Who carried out the ceremony?**

  The country's leading Church of England clergyman, the Archbishop of Canterbury, carried out the ceremony. His name was Geoffrey Fisher. It was he who placed the crown on the Queen's head.

- **What were the main events of Coronation Day?**

  There was a procession to Westminster Abbey for the ceremony. After, there was a procession back to Buckingham Palace. Next the Queen and her family appeared on the balcony. There was a flypast of aircraft. Later the Queen switched on a lighting display in London. Bonfires were lit all over the country.

- **Who turned up to watch?**

  Men, women and children from all parts of Britain and also from abroad flocked to London to watch the celebrations. It has been estimated that at least two million people lined the procession route.

- **What was the procession like?**

  The Queen travelled in a golden coach and all the other special guests were in carriages. There were over 13,000 members of the armed forces, some on foot, some on horseback. Twenty-nine marching bands played. The procession route was 11km long and took about two hours to walk. (See Generic sheet 1.)

- **What special decorations were there?**

  London was decorated with flags, arches, large crowns, banners, bunting, badges, shields and crests, model lions and unicorns. Red, white and blue were the main colours but gold and purple were also popular.

- **How did people all over the country see it happen?**

  People who could not get to London were able to watch the coronation on television. Some 27 million people did so at some time during the day. Large screen versions were shown in cinemas. Some watched outside television shops.

- **How did most ordinary people celebrate?**

  During the day, cities, towns and villages in Britain organised their own celebrations. There were street parties, dances, fancy dress parades, sports events, coronation queen and craft competitions, pageants and plays. These events went on long into the night.

Questions and answers

- **What do we mean by the term 'oral witness'?**

  An oral witness is someone who was alive when an event happened and can recall some things about it. Friends and family members may remember Coronation Day. Invite an oral witness into the classroom who will explain things carefully to children. Prepare questions beforehand. Make questions open-ended – for example, 'Where were you living on Coronation Day?' and 'What do you remember about the day?' (See Generic sheet 2 for a sample of witness accounts.)

- **What value are pictures, photographs and film?**

  Visual images appeal particularly to children in the early years. Encourage them to discuss what they can see. These resources should not only be used for observation but should lead to interpretation and follow-up. Who can be seen in the pictures? What are they doing?

- **What printed materials are available?**

  Many books were published on the coronation, including some specially written for children. Libraries can help to locate these. Newspapers and journals were full of nothing but the coronation in the summer of 1953. Replica copies of Coronation Day newspapers have been produced. Choose selected passages. Some simplification of the vocabulary may be needed.

- **What artefacts might be found for examination?**

  Set up an interest table or display feature in the classroom and appeal to children's families for as much Coronation Day memorabilia as possible. Items produced ranged from mugs to bread wrappers and from puzzles to cut-out models and pop-up books. Discuss what objects are made of, what they were used for and how much they cost.

Life in the 1950s

Food

The early 1950s saw an end to food rationing and other restrictions on goods like petrol and paper. Sweet rationing was lifted in time for the Coronation in 1953. Self-service stores and supermarkets began to develop as a contrast to the specialist grocers, bakers, butchers and small corner shops. Packaging design became brighter and bolder. Refrigerators became available and by 1955, 30 per cent of homes had their own. As a result, frozen foods became popular with Birds Eye fish fingers first appearing in 1955.

Housing

Lots of rebuilding needed to take place after the war, especially in cities that had suffered from bomb damage. Rows and rows of terraced houses were pulled down, many to be replaced by high-rise blocks of flats. Some people continued to live in prefabs – small, prefabricated buildings that were put up quickly to ease the housing shortage at the end of the war. Several new towns were built during the 1950s including Harlow and Cwmbran. People wanted to include all the latest gadgets in their homes – cookers, fridges, vacuum cleaners, washing machines and television sets. Many were made from the new types of brightly coloured plastics that were available. There were startling modern designs for furniture, fabrics and wallpaper. 'Do-it-yourself' magazines flooded the market.

Clothes and fashion

Certainly for the early part of the 1950s children's fashion was largely a scaled-down version of that worn by adults. School uniform for boys usually consisted of shirt with tie, pullover or blazer, short trousers, long socks and strong shoes. Long gabardine raincoats were popular and school caps. Pinafore dresses with blouses were worn by girls with thinner cotton dresses and cardigans in the summer. The advent of rock and roll and the 'Teddy boy' era revolutionised teenage fashion as did the arrival of versatile synthetic fibres like nylon, rayon and Terylene.

Transport and travel

Trams and trolley buses were still a feature of many towns and cities during the 1950s. Steam trains linked all parts of the country until the network was significantly reduced by the Beeching cutbacks of the early 1960s. The number of cars on the roads more than doubled during the decade although jams were few and parking restrictions more relaxed than they are today. Early cars were large with a great deal of chrome following the trend in America. But as petrol prices became important, smaller more economical models became popular. The Ford Popular could be bought for around £400 while the Morris Mini was around £500 when it appeared in 1959. Other models included the Hillman Minx, the Ford Anglia, the Morris Minor and the Vauxhall Victor. The Preston bypass, now part of the M6, was the first stretch of motorway and was opened in 1958. Parts of the M1 around London opened the following year. There was no speed limit until 1965 and no crash barriers between the carriageways.

Going to school

There were few working mothers in the 1950s so they were around more frequently to take children to and from school and look after them during the holidays. There were usually separate entrances for boys and girls and a common school sign stated, 'No parents past this point'. Most of today's curriculum subjects were taught in primary schools with a heavy emphasis on maths and English. There was little science teaching apart from nature study, craft as opposed to design and technology and no ICT. Exams like the 11+ determined which secondary schools children went to – grammar schools, technical schools or secondary moderns, as they were called. Young people could leave school at 15 or 16 and far fewer went on to further education at colleges and universities.

Life in the 1950s

Leisure time

The famous catch phrase used by the Prime Minister Harold Macmillan when he came to power in 1957 was that most people had 'never had it so good'. Work hours were certainly long but people could begin to look forward to more leisure time with bank holidays and two or three weeks of annual holiday each year. Seaside holidays became more popular with the growth of car sales, especially camping. Butlins had six large holiday camps in Britain. During the 1950s trips abroad on package holidays became an alternative. A 15-day visit to Majorca cost about £45. Two million people were travelling abroad on holiday by 1958.

Playing in the streets and in parks was much safer for children than it is now. Teenagers could visit the local coffee bar to play records (small plastic '45s') on the jukebox. Top recording artists were Cliff Richard, Elvis Presley, Chuck Berry, Tommy Steele and Perry Como. Watching the television, or 'gogglebox' as it was affectionately known, became a popular leisure time activity. Radio listening and visits to the cinema began to decline. By 1957 there were over seven million regular television viewers. A second channel, ITV, showing advertisements, started in 1955 but colour television was still over ten years in the future. Younger children enjoyed programmes like *Muffin the Mule* and *Andy Pandy* while there were adventure serials for the older ones like *Robin Hood* and *Bonanza*.

Newcomers

It was during the 1950s that many people sought refuge in Britain following the upheavals in Europe during the war. There were also a large number of immigrants arriving in Britain from the colonies and the Commonwealth. These included Caribbean countries, India, Pakistan, Kenya and other parts of Africa, China and Hong Kong. Many came as workers to fill the gaps in the British labour market. At the same time people also left Britain to settle in other parts of the world such as Australia and Canada.

The Festival of Britain

The festival consisted of events and exhibitions demonstrating Britain's achievements in industry, science and the arts. Held in 1951, it took place mainly in London but was also celebrated in other cities in Britain such as Belfast, Cardiff and Edinburgh. It was an opportunity for the country to show how it was breaking out from the austerity caused by the Second World War. Based around the Festival Hall alongside the River Thames, its most famous features were the Dome of Discovery and the Skylon – a thin piece of aluminium reaching up into the sky that seemed to float in the air. The event lasted for five months and was visited by some eight million people.

PHOTOCOPIABLE

The coronation of Queen Elizabeth II

> **History objectives**
> • To find out what happened on Coronation Day in 1953.
> • To understand how we know so much about it.

Resources

- Pictures of the Queen
- Photographs, pictures, prints, books, journals, newspapers, souvenirs and memorabilia of Coronation Day
- Witnesses for interview
- Equipment for recording and filming interviews (optional)
- Generic sheets 1, 2 and 5 (pages 89, 90 and 93)
- Activity sheets 1–3 (pages 99–101)

Starting points: *whole class*

Find out what the children know about the Queen. Show them her picture. What is her full name? Why did she become Queen? Have there been other queens with the same name before? Where does she live? How many different houses does she have? Where are they? Who is her husband? How many children does she have? How many grandchildren are there? What does she do? Discuss when the children have recently seen pictures of the Queen on television or in newspapers. Have any of them seen the Queen in real life? Where was this and why was the Queen there?

Then tell the children that in 2002 there was a celebration called the Golden Jubilee. It was to celebrate a very special day. They are going to find out more about this day, which took place just over 50 years ago. It was called Coronation Day and it was when the Queen officially became the ruler of the country. Explain that although Elizabeth II became Queen in February 1952 when her father died, it was not until June 1953 that her coronation took place. Say that events like this take a very long time to organise – in this case 16 months.

Show the children the route that the Coronation procession took (Generic sheet 1). Use the questions on Generic sheet 5 to help children acquire the information they need to know about Coronation Day. Then read out the quotes on Generic sheet 2.

Move on to discuss with the children why we know so much about the events surrounding Coronation Day. Talk about the meaning of evidence in an historical sense, especially the use of: people who were there; pictures, photographs and film; books, newspaper and journals and souvenirs or artefacts.

During this whole-class session try to arrange for someone who remembers the coronation to come into school and tell the children about it and answer their questions.

Group activities

Activity sheet 1

This sheet provides a basic writing frame for children who will need help and support to carry out interviews with adults who remember Coronation Day. The names of the interviewees should be written in the boxes. Space is provided for a sketch or photograph of the person being interviewed. Their comments should be written inside the speech bubbles. Encourage the children to find suitable adults who remember different aspects of the day, such as the service in Westminster Abbey, watching the procession or celebrations near home.

Activity sheet 2

This sheet is limited to one interviewee and provides specific questions for the children to ask. Questions appear on one side of the sheet and replies should be written opposite. Additional questions and the responses they bring can easily be added on the reverse of the sheet.

Activity sheet 3

This activity sheet is for more able children. They could work in pairs. It requires them to identify what they want to find out about the coronation and what possible questions they can ask an interviewee to obtain this information. Stress to children using this sheet that all questions should be open-ended to encourage the most detailed type of reply – for example, Where did you see the coronation? What celebrations do you remember near home?

Plenary session

Review the range of information that has been collected from the people interviewed by the children. Children can report back verbally or they may have recorded information on tape. It may also be possible to show a video recording of someone being interviewed.

Ideas for support

Support the information provided by witnesses, pictures, photographs and other printed sources by collecting fully labelled memorabilia for the classroom display.

Children will benefit from advice and guidance with interviewing skills and the ability to frame questions in an open-ended way.

Assistance will also be needed with technical equipment like tape recorders and video cameras if they are being used.

Ideas for extension

Encourage the children to find out more about the events surrounding the Queen's Silver Jubilee (1977) and Golden Jubilee (2002). Some of the events described by people interviewed about Coronation Day may be suitable for role play or drama activities.

Look to the future. When is the next coronation likely to take place? Can the children suggest what form it should take?

Linked ICT activities

Tell the children that they are going to interview each other about an event they have been to or remember from the past. Let them take turns to use a digital camera to take a photograph of someone in the class that they are going to interview. Ask each child in the class to write down on a piece of paper the event they would like to be interviewed about. This might be a holiday or a trip that they have been on or even a special family event. Put the children together in pairs and ask them to tell

each other about the event they would like to talk about. Let them decide between them what will be the best questions to ask each other.

Using a word processing program such as 'Talking Write Away', 'Textease' or 'Clicker 4', ask them to put together their list of questions that they are going to use for the interview. Attach the questions to a print-out of the photograph taken using the digital camera. The interview could then be taped and played to the rest of the class.

Name _____

I remember

What do people remember about Coronation Day? Draw their picture.

Name:

Name:

Name:

Name _____

I remember

Use these questions to find out about Coronation Day.

Person to be interviewed:

Name:

My questions:

The answers:

How old were you
then?

Where did you live?

How did you see the
coronation? Did you
watch on television or
were you there?

What do you remember
about the ceremony?

What do you remember
about the procession?

Did anything special
happen in your town?

PHOTOCOPIABLE

Name _____

I remember

You are going to use this sheet to interview someone about Coronation Day. Write down what you want to find out. The interview the person and write their answers down or use a tape recorder.

What I want to find out about the coronation:

Who I interviewed:

Date of interview:

My drawing of who I interviewed

What they said:

2

LESSON PLAN

The coronation of Queen Elizabeth II

Resources

- Generic sheets 3, 7 and 8 (pages 91, 95 and 96)
- Activity sheets 1–3 (pages 104–106)

Starting points: *whole class*

Start the session with some revision from the previous lesson about the types of evidence we can use to find out about what life was like for ordinary people in the decade between 1950 and 1960.

Talk about the use of eyewitness accounts from people who actually lived through those times. (The adults used as interviewees about Coronation Day may also prove to be a useful source of information here.) Discuss the use of newspapers, magazines, journals, comics and other printed sources from the period. Remind the children that there are photographs and pictures, videos produced for television, and early colour films that people have taken themselves. Also stress the importance of artefacts from the decade and other memorabilia associated with the times.

Then look at life in the 1950s through a series of theme headings, such as food, transport, clothes and fashion using whatever sources are readily available. (See Generic sheets 3, 7 and 8.)

Throughout this process encourage the children to make contrasts between life **then** and life **now**. (See activity sheets.) Make comparisons by considering **similarities** and **differences** and look for examples of both change and continuity.

Tell the children that they are now going to do an activity in which they look at the differences between life in the time of the coronation and life today. Before handing out the activity sheets, ask them to suggest some things that might have changed.

Group activities

Activity sheet 1
Drawings are provided in the 'then' column under the theme headings 'school', 'clothes', 'houses' and 'travel'. The children have to draw today's equivalents in the empty boxes in the 'now' column. Spend time discussing the variations between 'then' and 'now' when the task has been completed.

Activity sheet 2
Again empty boxes have to be completed on this activity sheet. This time the themes given are food, clothes, travel and houses. Sometimes the children have to complete the box on the 'now' side and sometimes on the 'then' side. They should do this with a drawing but are also required to describe what they have drawn in a sentence. After finishing the task they are encouraged to choose the change they like best and explain why.

Activity sheet 3
For the more able children, decisions have to be made about possible themes that can be used. Discussion may be necessary with this group beforehand so that reminders can be given about the topics covered, such as clothes, travel, housing and leisure time. The children will also need preparation work to help them refine the skill of comparing. Once they have completed the 'then' and 'now' boxes and written further information underneath, they are asked to itemise what things they think have changed most and what things they think have not changed at all. They are also asked to list the source materials they have used to gather information.

Plenary session

Review examples of children's drawings and writing from each of the three groups. Discuss the most significant changes that the children think have taken place. Using flash cards (pictorial or written) play the 'then' and 'now' game. You call out the name of something and the children have to answer 'then' or 'now'. Possible examples might be Ford Focus (now), holiday in Majorca for £45 (then), school caps and ties (then), DVD players (now), Morris Minor (then), Sky television (now), all steam trains (then).

Ideas for support

Presented with a wealth of different kinds of reference material, some children may get confused about where to search for information. Sort reference items such as pictures, photographs, newspaper items and artefacts into separate boxes or trays according to different topics like housing, clothes, transport and travel.

Revamp the home corner using aspects of a 1950s house. Stock the dressing-up box with 1950s clothes.

Have mixed ability pairs for active 'talk time' sessions on the carpet. Children have one minute to tell their partners about the changes that have happened between then and now.

Ideas for extension

When children have analysed the most significant changes that have occurred during the last 50 years ask them to go a stage further. Do they think the changes have been for the better or have they made matters worse? Would they have preferred to go to school in the 1950s, for example, or do they think it is better now?

Set calculations involving the pre-decimal money system used in the 1950s with its pounds (£), shillings (s) and pence (d). (There were 12 pennies to the shilling and 20 shillings to the pound.) (For those who are keen.)

Linked ICT activities

Talk to the children about all the different things we use now that help us around the home and we use everyday, such as a fridge, microwave, freezer, mobile phones, the internet, automatic washing machine and dryer. In preparation for Lesson 3, ask them what they think people would have had in their home in the 1960s. Ask them to make a list of all the things that we have to use now and all the things which they think would have been around then. Talk about what some of these things may have looked like. What kind of toys would children have had to play with?

Use the internet to begin to explore what life was like during the 1960s.

Name _____

Then and now

Look at the **then** pictures. Draw the **now** pictures. Talk about them.

THEN 1950s	NOW 2000s

School

School

Clothes

Clothes

Houses

Houses

Travel

Travel

Name _____

Then and now

Draw the missing pictures. Think carefully about **then** and **now**.
Then cut out all the pictures, stick them on another sheet of paper and write a caption for each one.

THEN – 1950S	NOW – 2000S

Food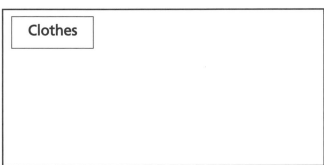

Food

Clothes

Clothes

Travel

Travel

Houses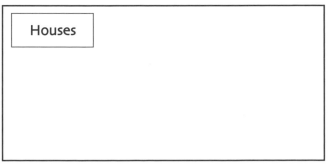

Houses

What change do you like best? Talk about it with a friend.

Name _____

Then and now

Choose some changes that have happened between **then** and **now**. Compare them by drawing pictures and writing sentences.

THEN — 1950S	NOW — 2000S

On the back of this sheet, write about:
- the things that have changed most;
- the things that have hardly changed at all;
- the sources you used to collect your information.

The coronation of Queen Elizabeth II

> **History objective**
> • To learn about the main events that have happened during the reign of Queen Elizabeth II.

Resources

- Large class timelines
- Class charts showing days of the week, months of the year, birthday dates and so on
- Family photographs, card, plastic wallets, washing line or string, pegs or clips
- Generic sheet 4 (page 92)
- Activity sheets 1–3 (pages 110–112)

Starting points: *whole class*

The main focus of the lesson is timelines. The timelines are related to work done on the 1950s and demonstrate how they can be used to improve children's sequencing skills and help them gain a greater sense and appreciation of time and chronology.

Before carrying out these specific tasks it will be necessary to prepare children with a number of practical activities. Work together to set up a diary of daily events so they can learn to sequence routines in the correct order, such as getting up, going to school, morning playtime, lunchtime, going home, having tea and going to bed. Spend time working on the order of the days of the week and the months of the year. Set up a large chart in the classroom that displays the order of children's birthdays throughout the year.

Work on key words and phrases used in association with the passing of time like 'past', 'present', 'future', 'before' and 'after', 'tomorrow', 'today' and 'yesterday', 'last week' and 'next week', 'earlier than' and 'later than', 'then' and 'now'. Try to be as precise as possible about time measures even at this stage and avoid vague phrases like 'a long time ago' and 'in the olden days'.

Ask the children, with parental permission, to bring to school a collection of three or four photographs of themselves taken at different stages in their lives. These can be arranged in the correct time order

starting with the present and going back in time. You might be brave enough to share in the activity by bringing in photographs of yourself at a variety of stages in your lifetime.

Children of this age should become familiar with seeing large timelines on classroom walls. Record on them events they have studied in history like those discussed in previous chapters. They should know by referring to the timeline, for example, that the Olympic Games of Ancient Greece came before the Gunpowder Plot and that Coronation Day happened after the Great Fire of London. At this stage, accurate sequencing is the important factor. Dates should be avoided, although some children will begin to appreciate the passing of time measured in centuries and then later in decades.

The children should know that timelines can be constructed in a number of different formats. They can be displayed horizontally with the present day shown on the right-hand side and time stretching away to the left. Alternatively, the line can be drawn vertically with 'now' shown at the base. Popular in some reference books for younger children are versions of the 'winding path' design that provides width for illustrations and gives the sense of a journey stretching away into the past.

Experiment with different techniques. Give the children playing-card sized photographs and pictures of buildings, characters in costume, types of transport and so on, to sort into the correct sequence. Alternatively, put large illustrations into plastic wallets and ask the children to arrange them on a ledge or shelf. Fix items to lengths of string with pegs or bulldog clips to create a 'washing line' effect. At all times encourage the children to talk about which clues help them most to make their decisions.

Then, using the information provided on Generic sheet 4, work with the children to create a timeline of the main events during the lifetime of Queen

Elizabeth II. Fix a long, wide strip of paper around the room and mark on it the approximate decades from the 1920s through to the 2000s. Count in tens – 1930s, 1940s, 1950s, and so on – with the children to see how many decades there are. Ask them to calculate how old the Queen is. Fix key dates from the Queen's life on to the timeline. This can be done starting with the Golden Jubilee celebrations and going back in time or at random (Coronation Day, Silver Jubilee, Wedding Day, first grandchild).

Extend the activity to make timelines of notable national and international events that have happened during the Queen's reign. These can be chosen by the children themselves depending on their particular interests, but some possibilities are given here and on the activity sheets to get them started. Again, stress the importance of getting the sequence correct and ensure it does not become a date-learning exercise. Those with sporting hobbies may want to include the dates, venues and key results of the Olympic Games, summer and winter versions, or the four-year cycles of the World Cups in football, rugby and cricket (see also Chapter 2 on the Olympic Games).

Group activities

Activity sheet 1
This activity sheet provides items associated with the reign of Queen Elizabeth II illustrated on the five screens of the television sets. The children have to draw themselves in the sixth. Then they have to cut out the pictures and correctly sequence the items to create their own timeline. No year references are necessary. Some assistance may be needed in order to keep their cutting and sticking as tidy as possible.

Activity sheet 2
On this activity sheet children are asked to cut out and place six events from the reign of Queen Elizabeth II into the correct sequence on the timeline provided. As a follow-up activity the children are asked to choose their favourite event and find out more about it.

Activity sheet 3
This activity sheet for more able children requires them to record the sequence of the six events given. The events are listed in headline form on the notice board complete with their dates. Discuss with the children first what possible forms the timelines

might take. They should have been shown examples of the horizontal, vertical and 'winding path' formats, but they may have alternative methods of their own. Space is provided for the timeline on the sheet but they may prefer to work on a larger piece of paper. As an extension the children are asked to find out more about their favourite event from the list.

Plenary session

Spend some time looking at examples of work from each of the three groups. The events used on each of the three activity sheets could be placed on a large class timeline using the 'washing line' method with a different child being asked to place events in the right sequence. Alternatively, the events could be shown on large cards with the children forming a human timeline. Back up the activity with lots of discussion about key events during the Queen's reign. Establish the following sequence solidly: Coronation, Silver Jubilee, My birth (the child), Golden Jubilee.

Discuss what other national and international events the children know about. Tell them about some that they don't know. You could choose from:
• England win the World Cup 1966
• Decimal coins first introduced 1969
• First colour televisions 1967
• Channel Tunnel opens 1994
• Britain joins the European Economic Community 1973
• Film ET first released 1985
• First man into space 1961
• Manchester United win the treble 1999
• Margaret Thatcher, first woman Prime Minister, 1979
• Berlin Wall comes down 1989
• Man on the moon 1969
• First test-tube baby 1978

Ideas for support

It is important that frequent preparation work on timelines is carried out with all children in the class before work is started on timelines specifically related to the Queen's reign during the last 50 years. Links can easily be made with other areas of the curriculum and timelining in history can be supported by work in the literacy hour, especially with the sequencing of familiar picture stories and nursery rhymes.

Support will be needed at home collecting photographs, family dates and so on.

Ideas for extension

Time is also a mathematical topic and opportunities should be found in this historical context to work with numbers. Counting in decades and later in centuries has already been mentioned. Go further. How many years has it been since 1970, 1980 and 1990?

Encourage the children to work on a personal evaluation sheet that can be used for this topic and earlier chapters in the book. What have they enjoyed learning? What has been most interesting? What has been least interesting? What would they like to learn more about?

Linked ICT activities

Show the children pictures of different types of technology and how things have changed over the years. Look at the types of telephones that were used during the 1970s and then how these have changed to the mobile phones we use today. Look at the changes in the mobile phones. Talk about the changes in televisions. Look at televisions in the 1970s and how these have changed to the wide screen ones we have today. Look at the types of games children play with – play stations and gameboy type games. Could the children imagine what it would be like not to have these games? Discuss how many of the items have become smaller, but with new features that make them much easier to use.

Look on the internet to find pictures of old technology, such as the old televisions and the old phones.

Create a technology timeline, adding to it when some of the key developments took place, such as the introduction of computers into the home, the use of the first mobile phone and the introduction of colour television.

Timelines

Look at these televisions. Draw yourself as a baby in the last one.
Cut them out. Put them in the order of when they happened.

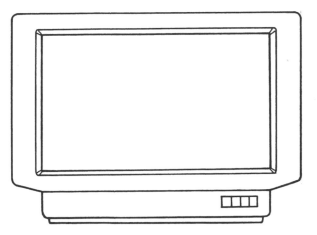

Draw yourself as a baby.

Timelines

Name _____

Here are some things that have happened since Elizabeth became Queen. Draw yourself as a baby in the empty box. Cut them out and put them in the right place on a timeline.

The Channel Tunnel opens

You as a baby

Coronation Day

The Golden Jubilee

First man on the moon

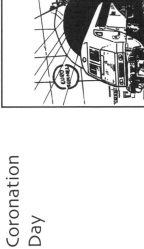

First motorway built

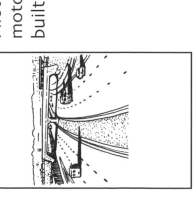

- With a friend choose your favourite event and find out more about it.

Timelines

Name _____

On the notice board are six headlines about events that happened during the reign of Queen Elizabeth II. On the timeline show the events in the right order. Label each one carefully. Choose an event on the timeline and do some research to find out more about it.

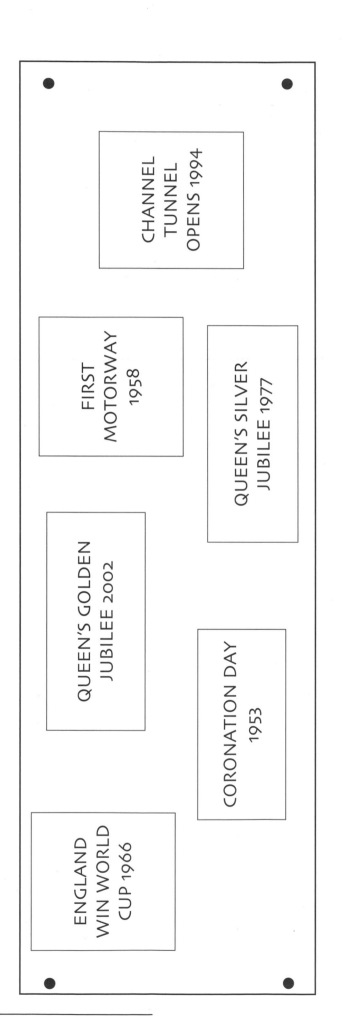

CHANNEL TUNNEL OPENS 1994

FIRST MOTORWAY 1958

QUEEN'S SILVER JUBILEE 1977

QUEEN'S GOLDEN JUBILEE 2002

CORONATION DAY 1953

ENGLAND WIN WORLD CUP 1966

1950　1960　1970　1980　1990　NOW

ACTIVITY SHEET 3